Negotiable Instruments
Law Unit

David Kobrin LLB(Hons), ACIS
Senior Lecturer in Law, Watford College
and
Vanessa Stott LLM(London) of Middle Temple, Barrister
Lecturer in Law, North East London Polytechnic

Anderson Keenan Publishing

First published 1980

Anderson Keenan Publishing Ltd
Imperial Buildings
56 Kingsway
London WC2B 6DX

© David Kobrin and Vanessa Stott 1980

ISBN 0 906501 15 6

Typeset by Columns
Printed and bound in Great Britain by
The Garden City Press Limited, Letchworth,
Hertfordshire SG6 1JS.

Contents

General Editor's Preface   vii

Authors' Preface   viii

1. **The Concept of Negotiability**   1

   Choses in Action — Negotiability — Some Important
   Negotiable Instruments — The Bills of Exchange Act, 1882

2. **The Form of a Bill**   9

   Operation of a Bill — Inland and Foreign Bills — Bills in a Set

3. **Definition of a Bill of Exchange**   4

4. **The Contractual Aspects of a Bill**   23

   Capacity to Contract — Consideration — Holders and their
   Rights — Signature — Forged and Unauthorised Signatures
   — Negotiation — Delivery — Inchoate Instruments

5. **Acceptance, Payment and Dishonour**   40

   Acceptance — Payment — Notice of Dishonour — Noting and
   Protesting — Damages in the Event of Dishonour —
   Acceptance and Payment for Honour

6. **Discharge of a Bill**   54

   Payment in Due Course — Payment of Accommodation Bills —
   When the Acceptor becomes the Holder — Express Waiver —
   Cancellation — Alteration of a Bill

7. **The Nature of a Cheque**   58

   Damages in the Event of Insolvency of Drawer's Bank —
   Determination of Banker's Authority — The Paying and
   Collecting Banks — The Form of a Cheque — Distinctions
   between Cheques and other Bills

8. **Crossings**   63

A General Crossing — A Special Crossing — Crossing 'Account
Payee' — Crossing 'Not Negotiable' — Crossings after Issue —
Scope of the Rules as to Crossings

9. **Relationship between Banker and Customer**   71

Opening the Accounts — Agency — The Customer's Duties
of Care — The Banker's Duties to the Customer

10. **The Protection of Bankers**   80

Protection of the Paying Banker — Protection of the
Collecting Banker

11. **Promissory Notes**   90

Inland and Foreign Notes — The Maker of a Note — Time
of Payment — Presentment for Payment — Distinctions
between Promissory Notes and Bills of Exchange — Bank
Notes — I.O.U.s

Index to Statutes   95

Index to Cases   97

General Index   99

General Editor's Preface

For many years the content of textbooks in law for students taking courses leading to professional qualifications in a variety of fields has been easy to ascertain. Authors have been able to analyse the syllabi of professional bodies and produce in one text chapters covering the various aspects of law required across a wide spectrum so that the student's requirements were met, though in some cases the text went beyond particular needs.

The situation today is very different. Professional bodies are increasingly allowing students to complete various stages of their professional qualifications on the basis of courses in colleges where the syllabus is designed by the lecturers involved who think differently as to topics to be studied and where the examination is set internally by the lecturer to reflect the course.

Thus there is a need for what might be called 'custom-built' text suitable to a particular approach by a lecturer. Anderson Keenan's Law Units are designed to allow a lecturer, having constructed his course, to recommend a number of suitable Units as reading for his students so that, by purchasing the relevant Units, the student and lecturer can make up, as it were, a wholly relevant text which covers what the student requires and does not necessitate the purchase of a general text with chapters some of which the student does not require.

In addition the Units are, it is hoped, practical in their approach so that the student for whom law is environmental is not required to study, as a lawyer would, topics which are on the fringe of legal knowledge. This, it is hoped, will tend to more efficient coverage of basic principles, leaving more time to deal with subjects which are fundamental to a particular qualification.

The Units could, it is felt, be extended to areas other than law. In this regard comments of lecturers would be welcome as leading to a further development of the Unit approach.

Denis Keenan

Authors' Preface

To students of business law, Negotiable Instruments is not always the most popular of the courses that they must take. This should not be so: once the student understands how bills of exchange actually work he or she should be able to master the subject. In this text, we have used one example which is developed and adapted as the book progresses, and this, with relevant cases integrated in the text, should enable the reader to grasp this very important and indeed interesting topic.

To those students of banking who are more familiar with the operation of bills of exchange we hope that we have been able to provide a comprehensive and readable statement of the law.

We are indebted to our publishers for their help and tolerance, especially to James Shepherd, to Juliet Shepherd for typing the manuscript so quickly and accurately, and last, but not least, to Alexandra Corrin for preparing the index.

D.L.K.
V.S.

March 1980

1 The Concept of Negotiability

Negotiable instruments have developed with the growth of trade. As the system of barter decreased, to be replaced by the notion of cash and money, so the concept of a written instrument evidencing the fact that money was owed (and would be paid) by one person to another developed. This written instrument which contained an undertaking that money would be paid at some determinable future time was a contract, and operated as a form of credit in that an immediate cash transaction was avoided and was replaced by an order stating that money would be paid in the future.

The law relating to negotiable instruments contains several concepts and principles which do not adhere to the basic common law rules of contract.

CHOSES IN ACTION

A right of action under a contract is that class of property known as a 'chose (thing) in action' and can be distinguished from tangible personal property, a 'chose (thing) in possession'. Share certificates, patents, trade marks, copyright, insurance policies and debts are all examples of choses in action. The term 'chose in action' is derived from the fact that a person is entitled to and, indeed, can only bring an action before the court to claim or enforce his right. This is in contrast to a tangible moveable such as a pen, a 'chose in possession', a person being able to enforce his right by obtaining physical possession and not necessarily having to take legal proceedings.

At common law a person not a party to a contract is not entitled to enforce the contract. This fundamental principle was extended by common law to forbid a person, to whom the benefit of a contract had been transferred or assigned, to sue on it in his own name. Equity, which evolved in the Court of Chancery from the late fourteenth century, did, however, recognise and would enforce the transfer of the benefit of a contract, but the transferee in equity was required to take the benefit of a contract subject to defects in title on the part of the transferor.

In other words, the transferee (assignee) could not obtain any greater rights than those enjoyed by the transferor (assignor). Therefore any right of set-off or defence of which the debtor could have availed himself against the transferor could similarly be used against the transferee so long as those rights or defences existed before the debtor was notified of the assignment. This restriction upon the full enjoyment of the transferee to the chose in action assigned to him (in other words, his inability to obtain any better rights than the transferor) is indicated by the phrase 'assignment is subject to equities'.

Example

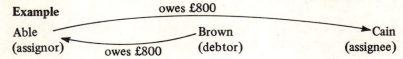

It would seem to be convenient for Able to assign to Cain the debt of £800 owing by Brown to Able. At common law Cain could not sue Brown in his own name, but would need to obtain Able's assistance and sue in the name of Able; if Able refused then, at common law, Cain would have no rights against Brown. But equity would compel Able to lend his name in an action brought by Cain, the assignee, so long as notice of the transfer had been given to Brown.

However, it could be that Able owed Brown, say, £100 in respect of goods delivered before the debt was assigned to Cain. The Court of Chancery would recognise this 'equity', the right of set-off, by holding that Cain's right to £800 against Brown was subject to Brown's right of set-off in the amount of £100 against Cain, who would only be required therefore to pay £700 to Cain.

This general principle still applies, despite the intervention of statute law (s 25, Judicature Act, 1873, now s 136, Law of Property Act, 1925) which, at last, gave the blessing of the common law to the transferee of a chose in action, entitling him to sue the debtor *in his own name* in the courts of common law; that assignment is subject to equities, however, is still the general rule both in equity and at common law.

A bill of exchange is in essence a contract and a chose in action. It is a contract which evidences that money is owed and contains an order for that money to be paid at some future time.

Bills of exchange were recognised by the custom and usage of traders and merchants as a special and distinctive type of chose in action as early as the fourteenth century: but their recognition by the Common Law Courts had to wait until the early seventeenth century. Merchants frequently used such bills not only as evidence of a debt between the immediate parties to a contract but also as an instrument of value to offer to a third party in lieu of an immediate cash payment.

NEGOTIABILITY

Negotiability is peculiar to a small class of contractual instruments which include bills of exchange, promissory notes (and thus bank notes), cheques, bearer shares, bearer debentures, dividend warrants and Treasury bills.

2

The basic characteristics of a negotiable instrument are:

(1) That the document must be transferable by mere delivery or by indorsement and delivery.

(2) That a legal title will pass free from defects in title provided that the *bona fide* purchaser for value has no notice of any defects in title on the part of the transferor.

(3) That notice of the transfer need not be given to the person obliged to pay.

We now consider each of these characteristics in more detail.

(1) Transfer by delivery

If an instrument is to be used frequently it is essential that its use is not combined with complex systems of notification and registration.

The merchants and traders transferred bills of exchange (the most important of all negotiable instruments) made payable to the bearer of that bill by mere delivery. Bills made payable to a specified person were transferred by that person signing his name on the bill and then delivering it to a third party. Mercantile custom and, later, the common law recognised these two methods of transfer as valid and effective for all forms of negotiable instrument. No further formalities were required.

(2) Legal title free from equities

From the seventeenth century the common law, in deference to mercantile custom, recognised the right to transfer negotiable instruments, but, as we have seen, denied this right to most other forms of chose in action.

The transfer of the benefit to a chose in action was, it will be remembered, recognised in equity, but such a transfer was subject to any defects in title on the part of the transferor. Thus any right of counter-claim or set-off which existed in relation to a debt would continue to exist notwithstanding the (equitable) assignment of the right to enforce that debt to a third party.

Statute law in the form of the Judicature Act, 1873, finally came to recognise legal assignment (of instruments other than negotiable instruments) and now upholds a legal assignment of the benefit of a contractual right. Such a transfer does not, however, provide the transferee with a title which is free from the defects in title (if any) which exist in relation to the transferor.

It was essential to the needs of the trading community that a bill of exchange could be transferred free from such defects or equities on the part of the transferor. Provided that value was given by the transferee for the bill

3

and provided that the transferee had no notice of any defects in title he would acquire the bill free from equities. Thus, referring to the example on page 2, had the transfer of Brown's indebtedness from Able to Cain taken place in the form of a negotiable instrument, then, so long as value had been given for the bill by Cain and he was unaware of Brown's right of set-off against Able, he would acquire a right to the full £800.

This is the major distinguishing feature between all negotiable instruments and other choses in action.

(3) Notice

Notice of the fact of transfer need not be given to the person stated in the bill of exchange as being obliged to pay the amount specified in the bill. This procedure is in marked contrast both to equitable transfers, where notice, although no longer mandatory, is essential on practical grounds, and to assignments under s 136 of the Law of Property Act, 1925 (replacing s 25 of the Judicature Act, 1873), which stipulates that express notice, in writing, of the assignment of all debts and other legal choses in action must be given to the debtor, trustee or other person who holds the funds assigned. Thus under s 136 the debtor at any given moment in time will know who is entitled to the fund he is holding.

The person obliged to pay by virtue of the order written in the bill of exchange will not know who will (or may) demand payment from him. Payment may be demanded either by the person specified in the bill or it may be demanded by the person to whom the bill has been negotiated.

The characteristics of negotiation themselves define a negotiable instrument. Any instrument which requires more than mere delivery (or indorsement and delivery) to effect a transfer of entitlement cannot be a negotiable instrument. Share certificates (in contrast to share warrants) require the completion of a share transfer form and re-registration in the name of the new holder to effect a legal transfer. Thus share certificates are not negotiable instruments. Similarly, an instrument which does not pass free from possible defects in title is not a negotiable instrument. The bank as legal holder of a customer's life assurance policy by way of security might discover that its customer had mis-stated his or her age. Incorrect information as to age with respect to life assurance policies will not void the contract but will affect the value of the policy to the bank, in that it may alter the amount recoverable under the policy. The bank cannot claim, should it choose to surrender the policy, that it is not affected by the discovery of the correct age. There is also a requirement that notice of assignment of a life policy must be given to the relevant life office. Thus life assurance policies are not negotiable instruments: title to a life assurance policy cannot be transferred free from previous defects in title, and notice is required to be given for the transaction to qualify as being valid.

SOME IMPORTANT NEGOTIABLE INSTRUMENTS

(1) Bills of exchange

A bill of exchange is an order, in writing, that a certain sum of money will be paid in the future. It operates as a form of credit in that the order provides that payment will be made at a fixed or determinable future time and obviates the need to pay cash immediately. The use of a bill, as opposed to an outright delay in payment, enables its recipient to transfer the entitlement to the order to one of his own creditors.

Although the form of a bill will be discussed in detail in Chapter 2, an example which develops the situation discussed already on page 2 will be helpful. Thus taking the following example of a bill of exchange:

---

                 25 Long Street
                     London
£800   10 October 1980

 Four months after date pay to Cain or order the sum of
 eight hundred pounds
        (Signed)
          Able

To:
 Brown
 81 Short Street
 Salisbury

Here, Able the drawer of the bill, has directed Brown, the drawee, who presumably owes at least £800 to Able, to pay that sum of money to Cain, the payee, instead, in order to settle Able's indebtedness to Cain: the payment in this example is to be made by Brown at some definite future time, though payment could alternatively be required to be made as and when demanded by Cain; in other words 'on demand'.

The bill operates therefore as a means of assigning the debts shown in our earlier example, with all the advantages to the parties of a negotiable instrument.

Bills of exchange are increasingly important as a means of allowing credit to the buyer of goods and yet, through the commercial banking machinery, enabling the seller to be paid promptly. Thus:

```
                                              25 Long Street
                                                   London
       £800                                  10 October 1980

             Four months after date pay to my order the sum of eight
             hundred pounds
                              (Signed)
                                           Able
       To: Brown
           81 Short Street
           Salisbury
```

Brown has bought £800 worth of goods from Able and no doubt will be prepared to accept a liability to meet payments of this bill in four months' time. Meanwhile, assuming that it is satisfied as to Brown's creditworthiness, a bank will probably be willing to purchase or 'discount' the 'accepted' bill immediately from Able for, say, £740. Therefore Able, the seller, will be paid promptly, Brown has four months in which to pay the £800, and the bank has earned £60.

These bills also operate as a means of avoiding foreign exchange controls on cash in that a bill may be proffered as payment with respect to a number of transactions all over the world. If the debtor is in the United Kingdom and the ultimate creditor is in the United Kingdom, then the intervening world-wide transactions will not have involved any cash transactions. So currency restrictions, controls and rates of exchange become irrelevant.

Bills of exchange are themselves a form of security. They prevent the need for large amounts of cash to be carried by any person and, in that a bill may be sent abroad in several parts, they avoid the possibility of an entire bill being lost in the post.

(2) Promissory notes

A promissory note is a development of the simple I.O.U. Unlike the I.O.U., however, it is a negotiable instrument and it contains a promise by the person drawing it up to pay some other person either in the future or on demand.

There are strong similarities to bills of exchange, but, unlike bills, promissory notes never have more than two parties. Furthermore, with a bill of exchange the party who writes the order is not the person who is going to pay the sum ordered in the bill. The person who draws up a promissory note will be the debtor.

A bank note is a promissory note and therefore a negotiable instrument. The Bank of England promises to pay to the bearer the amount stated in the note on demand. Such notes are so frequently used that they have become recognised as 'cash', and will be legal tender for the amount stated.

(3) Cheques

Cheques are a particular type of bill of exchange. The debtor or drawee named in the cheque must always be a banker and a cheque is always payable on demand.

Thus if we take the first example of a bill of exchange (see page 5) and substitute the words 'on demand' for 'Four months after date', and 'Brown Bank Ltd' for 'Brown' as the drawee of the bill, we have a cheque.

The enormous increase in use of cheques has necessitated that bankers obtain some protection in the event of their paying the sum ordered to a person who is not actually entitled to that sum but who represents himself as being entitled. The technical requirement of negotiating cheques to bankers and between bankers have for the same reasons been reduced considerably, compared with other bills of exchange.

A document bearing great similarity to a cheque is a dividend warrant which is an order drawn by a company on its bank (usually on a separate Dividend Account) for the payment of dividends to shareholders out of profits earned by the company. The dividend warrant is nearly always drawn in the form of a cheque and will then be a valid cheque in all respects.

(4) Bearer shares and bearer debentures

Shares and debentures are instruments peculiar to companies. A share certificate is evidence of ownership of a part of a company. A share certificate may be issued in the name of a specific person or may be issued to bearer. Bearer share certificates, known as share warrants, are negotiable instruments.

A debenture is a document evidencing a loan to a company. A debenture may state the name of the lender as the person entitled to repayment of the loan (and meanwhile to interest on that loan) or may state that either of these payments are to be made to the bearer of the debenture certificate. Bearer debentures are negotiable instruments.

The title to both bearer shares and bearer debentures passes by mere delivery.

That bearer debentures are treated as negotiable illustrates the point that the categories of negotiable instruments are not closed and the courts will give effect to the universal recognition by the business community that a particular category of instrument is negotiable.

BECHUANALAND EXPLORATION CO. v. LONDON TRADING BANK [1898] 2 QB 658

The company secretary of Bechuanaland Exploration Company fraudulently deposited some bearer debentures owned by his company with the bank. The bank took the debentures in good faith and used them as security for loans to the company secretary.

It was *held*, on evidence being given, that mercantile custom treated bearer debentures as negotiable and transferable by delivery, and that the bank was entitled to them as against the Bechuanaland Exploration Company.

THE BILLS OF EXCHANGE ACT, 1882

The law relating to bills of exchange was codified by the very distinguished draftsman Sir Mackenzie Chalmers as the Bills of Exchange Act, 1882, to this day the principal source of law on the topic. Therefore all references to 'the Act' in the succeeding chapters and all sections cited will, unless otherwise stated, indicate the 1882 statute.

2 The Form of a Bill

The definition of a bill does not require it to be in any particular form.

OPERATION OF A BILL

A bill may typically take the form of our first example (see page 5), which illustrates a bill payable at a fixed future time.

> Cain will be entitled to claim payment from Brown on 10 February 1981 (assuming that Brown has accepted liability on the bill). If before that date Cain sells the bill to Mark and constitutes Mark the valid holder of the bill by signing his own name on the back of the bill, i.e. indorsing the bill, and ordering that payment should now be made to Mark, then Mark must present that bill to Brown for payment on 10 February 1981.

Alternatively, a bill may be expressed to be payable a certain number of days after 'sight', i.e. after the first sighting of the bill by the drawee. Thus:

```
                                                  25 Long Street
                                                          London

 £800                                           31 December 1980

 At 90 days after sight pay to the order of Cain eight hundred
 pounds
                          (Signed)

                                 Able

 To: Brown
     81 Short Street
     Salisbury
```

LU—NI—2 **

The 90-day period runs from the sighting of the bill by Brown. Cain will be able to claim the £800 from Brown on the 90th day not including the day when Brown sighted the bill.

Instead of the bill being made payable to a named payee it may be drawn payable to bearer, thus:

25 Long Street
London

£800   15 April 1980

Twelve months after date pay to bearer the sum of eight hundred pounds

          (Signed)

               Able

To: Brown
     81 Short Street
     Salisbury

Brown, the initial holder of this bill, may negotiate it to Cain simply by handing over or 'delivering' the bill. Alternatively Brown may specify on the reverse of the bill that the amount stated is now payable to Cain or to the order of Cain. Thus a bill which was originally expressed payable to bearer is made payable to a specified person.

Where a bill is made payable to a specified person or to his order, that person may convert the specially indorsed bill into a bill payable to bearer by simply signing his name on the reverse of the bill. Such an indorsement is referred to as an 'indorsement in blank'. The signature of Cain on the reverse of the bill below the special indorsement will convert the bill into a bearer bill, and so on.

If a bill is made payable to Cain in that on the face of the bill can be found the words 'Pay Cain the sum of eight hundred pounds' with no reference to the bill being payable to the order of Cain, he may nevertheless treat the bill as if it is payable to himself or to his order at his option (s 8(5)).

A bill which is made payable to or to the order of Cain on its face may take the following form on its reverse side:

```
(1)          Pay to Mark          Cain
                                  (Signature)

(2)          Pay to or to the order of Quentin

                                  Mark
                                  (Signature)

(3)          Quentin
             (Signature)
```

(1) Is a specific indorsement of the bill by Cain to Mark. Mark is now the person entitled to claim payment when the bill matures. Mark can negotiate the bill notwithstanding the absence of the words 'or order'.

(2) Is a specific indorsement by Mark to Quentin.

(3) Quentin's signature operates as a blank indorsement and thus the bill becomes payable to bearer. Any subsequent holder of the bill can specify to whom the bill is payable. Thus a bill can be converted back into an order bill payable to a specified person or to the order of that person.

INLAND AND FOREIGN BILLS

S 4 provides that an inland bill is one which is or on the face of it purports to be either

(a) Both drawn and payable within the British Islands, or

(b) Drawn within the British Islands upon some person resident therein.

Any other bill is said to be a foreign bill.

The British Islands for the purposes of this Act is stated to mean any part of the United Kingdom of Great Britain and (Northern) Ireland and the Islands of Man, Guernsey, Jersey, Alderney and Sark and any adjacent islands being part of the dominions of the Monarch.

Under (a) a bill must be both drawn and payable within the British Islands in order to qualify as an inland bill. Thus the address supplied by the drawer and the address given to indicate where the bill is payable must both be within the British Islands. Thus:

If Able, giving his address as London, draws a bill on Brown in Rome payable to Cain in Birmingham, then it is an inland bill, but if Able gives his address as in Canada, or if the bill is stated to be payable to Cain in Canada the bill will not qualify as an inland bill under (a).

Alternatively it is provided under (b) that to qualify as an inland bill it must be drawn within the British Islands upon some person resident within the British Islands. The drawee must therefore be resident within the British Islands. If therefore Brown's address is given as France then the bill would not qualify as an inland bill under (b).

Unless, however, it is apparent and clear on the face of the bill that it is a foreign bill, the holder may treat the bill as an inland bill.

The significance of this distinction between inland and foreign bills will be seen in more detail later (Chapter 5) with respect to the requirements of acceptance of bills of exchange. Acceptance is the process whereby the drawee of a bill becomes primarily liable to pay the sum stated in the bill. Acceptance takes the form of the signature of the drawee. Up until the time when the drawee accepts the bill by adding his signature to it, it is the drawer and any indorsers of the bill who are primarily liable on the bill. If a foreign bill is dishonoured for non-acceptance an official note of the dishonour must be obtained. This procedure is known as noting and protesting and is carried out by a notary public.

Where a bill which has not previously been dishonoured for non-acceptance is presented for payment and payment is refused the bill is said to be dishonoured for non-payment. When a foreign bill is dishonoured for non-payment an official note of the dishonour must be obtained. Thus the bill will be protested for non-payment.

BILLS IN A SET

Bills of exchange may be issued in a set. Where a bill is drawn in a set each part must be numbered and must contain a reference to the existence of the other parts. It is only the totality of the parts which constitutes a bill (s 71(1)). Thus:

```
                                              25 Long Street
                                                     London
        £800                                10 October 1980
           Sixty days after sight pay this first of exchange (second and
           third of the same tenor and date being unpaid)* to the order
           of Cain, the sum of eight hundred pounds
                               (Signed)
        To: Brun
            24 rue Rouge                     Able
            Geneva
```

*The wording of the second part will read 'sixty days after sight pay this second of exchange (first and third of the same tenor and date being unpaid), etc.', and the third part will be with appropriate substitutions.

The different parts of the bill are posted separately, thus operating as a security device; the loss of any one part will not complicate matters since Brun, the drawee, can accept any part. He must take care, however, to accept only one part, since if he accepts two parts he may have to pay both if they fall into the hands of different holders.

Bills in a set are only to be found in international trade and are rare even there since the growth of the banker's commercial credit as a means of financing this trade.

Where the holder of a set indorses two or more parts to different persons he is liable as indorser on every part. Every subsequent indorser is liable on the part he has indorsed as if it were a separate bill (s 71(2)).

The acceptance by the drawee of a bill issued in a set may be written on any part of the set but must be written on one part only. If the drawee accepts more than one part and each of those accepted parts comes into the hands of a holder in due course (see page 25) the drawee is liable on every part as if it were a separate bill. The acceptor must be sure that he pays against delivery of the accepted part only, otherwise if he pays an unaccepted part he will also be liable to pay the holder in due course of the accepted part (s 71(5)).

When the acceptor has paid the holder of the accepted part of the bill drawn in set that part is discharged by payment and the whole bill is discharged.

3 Definition of a Bill of Exchange

In its simplest form a bill of exchange involves three parties:

(1)   The drawer (Able), the person who draws up the bill which contains an order that some person receives money and some other person pays money.

(2)   The drawee (Brown), the person to whom the order to pay is given: the payer.

(3)   The payee (Cain), the person who is to receive the sum stated in the order written by the drawer: payment to be collected from the drawee.

A bill of exchange is defined in s 3 Bills of Exchange Act, 1882 (hereinafter referred to as 'the Act') as 'An unconditional order in writing, addressed by one person to another, signed by the person giving it, requiring the person to whom it is addressed to pay on demand or at a fixed or determinable future time a sum certain in money to or to the order of a specified person, or to bearer'.

This definition can be broken down into eight basic requirements:

(1)   An unconditional order

(2)   in writing

(3)   addressed by one person to another

(4)   signed by the person giving it

(5)   requiring the person to whom it is addressed

(6)   to pay on demand or at a fixed determinable future time

(7)   a sum certain in money

(8)   to or to the order of a specified person or to bearer.

An instrument which does not comply with these conditions is not a bill of exchange.

14

Considering each of these basic requirements in further detail:

(1) An unconditional order

The order stated in the bill must be unconditional. It must simply state that a certain amount of money will be paid, and no conditions may be attached to the payment of the money. The requirement that goods given in consideration for the bill are of merchantable quality or fit for their purpose as a condition to be fulfilled before the amount stated will be paid denies the order the status of a bill of exchange. S 3(2) provides that an instrument which orders any act to be done in addition to the payment of money is not a bill of exchange.

BAVINS JUNIOR & SIMS v. LONDON AND SOUTH WESTERN BANK [1900] 1 QB 270

An instrument which stated 'Pay to J. Bavins Junior & Sims the sum of £69 7s provided the receipt form at the foot hereof is duly signed, stamped and dated' was *held* not to constitute a bill of exchange, payment being dependent upon a condition being fulfilled. On the other hand, in *Nathan* v. *Ogdens Ltd* (1905) 94 LT 126 the instrument contained the words 'the receipt at the back hereof must be signed'. This instrument was *held* to be directed to the payee, not the drawee, so the order to the drawee was unconditional and the instrument a valid bill of exchange.

By s 3(3) an order to pay money out of a particular fund is conditional (since that fund might be inadequate at the date due for payment) but an unqualified order to pay combined with either (a) an indication of the particular fund out of which the drawee is to reimburse himself or a particular account to be debited with that amount, or (b) a statement of the transaction which gives rise to the bill is unconditional, and therefore a valid bill of exchange. Thus an order stating 'pay £10,000 out of the proceeds of sale of my house' is conditional, but 'pay £10,000 and debit my No. 2 account' is a valid bill, since the reference to the particular account merely indicates the account to be debited and the holder is not relying upon that particular fund being sufficient to meet the order.

(2) In writing

The bill must be in writing. S 2 provides that the words 'in writing' include print. There is no requirement in the Act as to the surface on which the writing must be; hence seemingly endless legal jokes, writing cheques on eggs, paving stones, College Rag Queens and even a dead shark! The Coinage Act, 1870 forbids a bill in metallic form.

(3) Addressed by one person to another

A bill is drawn up by the person referred to as the drawer. The drawer will address his order to the drawee.

S 6 provides that the drawee must be named or otherwise indicated in the bill with reasonable certainty. There may be two or more drawees named in the bill but if their liability is expressed to be in the alternative (that one or other of them may be liable) or in succession (that one is only liable after the other) the instrument will not constitute a bill of exchange. Where there are two or more drawees they may be partners, but in any event they must be jointly liable.

Where in a bill the drawer and drawee are the same person or where the drawee is a fictitious person or a person not having capacity to contract, the holder may treat the instrument at his option either as a bill of exchange or as a promissory note. The most important example is a banker's draft, which in form resembles a bill of exchange but may be treated as a promissory note by the holder. The branch bank, at the request of and on debiting the account of its customer, issues a draft drawn on its Head Office. In other words, the bank has made an order on itself in favour of the person to whom its customer wishes payment to be made; from the payee's viewpoint this is more satisfactory than a cheque signed by an individual drawer, and it is commonly used in the purchase of valuable items such as houses and motor vehicles. Thus:

> The drawer of the bill is Able and he is writing an order to Brown. Brown is the person to whom the order is addressed.

(4) Signed by the person giving it

The bill must be signed by the drawer. In our example Able must sign the bill if it is to constitute a valid binding order.

(5) Requiring the person to whom it is addressed

The person to whom the bill is addressed is the drawee. In our example the drawee is Brown.

(6) To pay on demand or at a fixed or determinable future time

The drawer will require the drawee to pay the amount stated in the bill:

(a)   When that amount is demanded from him, or

(b)   At a fixed future date, or

16

(c)   At a determinable future date.

S 10 describes a bill payable on demand as one which is expressed to be payable:

  (i)   On demand, or

  (ii) At sight, or

  (iii) On presentation.

'At sight or on presentation' means when the bill is sighted by the drawee or presented to him for acceptance. A bill which expresses no time for payment, for instance a cheque, is also payable on demand. Thus:

> If Able draws up the bill and states that payment will be made on demand, when Cain presents the bill for payment to Brown, Brown, if he has accepted liability on the bill, is obliged to pay to Cain the amount stated in the bill.

By s 10(3) where a bill is accepted or indorsed when it is overdue it shall, as regards the acceptor who so accepts, or any indorser who so indorses it, be deemed a bill payable on demand.

  S 11 describes a bill payable at a determinable future time as one expressed to be payable:

  (i)   At a fixed period after date or sight; 'sight' here means when the drawee signifies his acceptance. Commonly, bills are expressed to be payable on a specific date or else they are made payable 30 or 60 or 90 days after sight or issue.

  (ii) On or at a fixed period after the occurrence of a specified event which is certain to happen, though the time of happening may be uncertain.

The proviso to s 11 states: 'An instrument expressed to be payable on a contingency is not a bill and the happening of the event does not cure the defect.' Thus a distinction needs to be made between an event which is bound to happen and one which may not. Thus a bill drawn payable '60 days after Jack Smith's death' will be a valid bill, but one drawn payable '60 days after George Jones' marriage' is invalid because the marriage is not certain to take place. Furthermore, the fact that George Jones does, in fact, marry will make no difference, so we are told by the proviso.

In this case it was *held* that a document payable 'On or before December 31st 1956' was not a bill of exchange because of uncertainty and contingency in the time of payment.

The Banking and Financial Dealings Act, 1971 prescribes the time allowed for presenting a bill payable at a determinable future time. A bill is due and payable in all cases on the last day of the time of payment as fixed by the bill or, if that is a non-business day, on the succeeding business day. Thus a bill drawn payable 30 days after issue must be presented for payment on the 30th day or, if that is a non-business day, on the succeeding business day.

Non-business days are described by s 92 to include (a) Sunday, Good Friday and Christmas Day, and (b) Bank holidays. Any other day is expressly referred to as a business day.

Where a bill is payable at a fixed period after sight, date or the happening of a specified event, the time of payment is determined by excluding the day from which the time is to run and including the day of payment. Thus if a bill is payable 30 days after sight, the day the drawee 'sights' the bill does not constitute the first of the 30 days. The 30-day period runs from the following day and the bill falls due for payment on the 30th day.

With respect to a 'time' bill the date of maturity of a bill (that is, the date as specified in the order when payment is due) is vital. If a bill continues in circulation after the date of maturity the holder of it will take subject to any defects in title at the date of maturity. From the date of maturity no person can acquire or give a better title to the bill than that enjoyed by the person from whom he took it (s 36).

Bills payable on demand are not overdue until they have been in circulation for an unreasonable amount of time. What is unreasonable will depend upon the custom and usage of a bill in each instance.

S 13(2) provides that a bill is not invalid by reason only that it is antedated or post-dated or dated on a Sunday.

If the date is omitted from a bill any holder may insert the true date. Furthermore, if in good faith and by mistake he inserts the wrong date, but the bill comes into the hands of a holder in due course (see Chapter 4) the bill is payable as if the date inserted had been the true date.

(7) A sum certain in money

The sum ordered to be paid by the bill must be a sum certain in money. This requirement of the definition is satisfied notwithstanding that the sum ordered is required to be paid either

(1) With interest, or

(2) By stated instalments, or

(3) By stated instalments with a provision that upon default in payment of any instalments the whole sum shall be due, or

(4) According to an indicated rate of exchange to be ascertained as directed by the bill (s 9(1)).

Where there is a sum expressed in words and also in figures and there is a discrepancy between the two, the sum denoted by the words is the amount payable (s 9(2)). Thus words prevail over figures, but a bank will usually return a cheque unpaid, in these circumstances, marked 'words and figures differ'.

By s 9(3) where a bill is expressed to be payable with interest then unless the instrument states otherwise, interest runs from the date of the bill, and if the bill is not dated, then from the actual date of issue.

In the past the courts have taken the view that if no rate of interest is stated then 5 per cent will be presumed, but many authorities accept that bills do not carry interest unless they expressly provide for it.

The amount as stated in the bill can only be altered with the consent of all the parties. If a person alters the amount to be paid without the consent of any party to the bill that party is discharged from liability (see Chapter 6).

(8) To or to the order of a specified person or to bearer

A bill may be made payable to a specified person or it may be drawn payable to bearer.

(a) Specified person

In our example Able has specified the person entitled to be paid as Cain. Thus the bill is payable to a specified person.

A bill is not invalid by virtue of there being no specified payee but where a bill is not payable to bearer it is essential that the payee is named or otherwise indicated in the bill with reasonable certainty (s 7).

NORTH & SOUTH INSURANCE CORP. v. NATIONAL PROVINCIAL BANK LTD [1936] 1 KB 328

It was *held* that an instrument made out to 'Pay cash or order' was not a bill of exchange. 'Cash' does not fulfill the requirement of a 'specified person or to bearer'. (The instrument was *held* to be a valid order as between a bank and its customer.)

A bill may be payable to two or more payees jointly or it may be made payable in the alternative to one of two or one of several. This is in marked contrast to the provision relating to drawees (see heading (3) above).

Where a person wishes to draw cash from his bank account he may write a 'pay self' cheque for the amount; thus the drawer and the payee may be the same person; again the bill may be drawn in favour of the drawee. Where, for instance, a customer wishes to pay his bank for, say, insurance services he will write a cheque on his account (the bank being drawee) in favour of the bank.

A bill may be made payable to the holder of an office for the time being. Thus a bill may be made payable to the 'Treasurer of Midshire Council' or the 'Collector of Taxes'. A bill may also be made payable to the order of a specified person. Thus:

> Able may state that the bill is payable 'To Cain or order'. Cain, even in the absence of the latter words, would be entitled to transfer the bill to, for example, Mark, and write on the back of the bill that he is ordering payment to be made to Mark, and not himself. The words 'or order' are simply an indication that the bill is negotiable. All bills are negotiable unless there is an express provision which restricts the right to transfer the bill.

Hence a bill may be drawn payable to one of three types of payee:

(i) To pay a specified person; in our example 'Pay Cain'.

(ii) To pay a specified person or to pay to his order; in our example 'Pay Cain or order' or 'Pay to or to the order of Cain'.

(iii) 'To bearer'.

(b) Bearer

By s 8(3) a bill is payable to bearer, which is expressed to be so payable or on which the only or last indorsement is an indorsement in blank (see Chapter 2). Thus the bearer bill may have been drawn originally as an order bill.

Where a payee is a fictitious or non-existing person the bill may be treated as payable to bearer (s 7(3)), and no indorsement will be required for negotiation of the bill. The Act, however, fails to define 'fictitious', and this has given rise to a certain amount of litigation.

When deciding whether the payee is fictitious the test applied by the court is 'did the drawer intend the person named to take the money through the bill which he has drawn?' If the answer is 'no' and the payee's name was inserted by way of pretence then the payee will be 'fictitious' even though he is an existing person.

BANK OF ENGLAND v. VAGLIANO BROS [1891] AC 107

A fraudulent clerk of Vagliano Bros drew up bills inserting his employer as the drawee, P & Co., as payee and forging the signature of the drawer. The purported drawer and P & Co. were frequent customers of Vagliano Bros and the transaction therefore appeared to be feasible. The clerk forged P & Co.'s indorsement thus indicating that the bills were payable to bearer and obtained payments for himself from the Bank of England. The question to be decided by the court was whether the bills, from their inception, were payable to bearer. If they were, the debit of Vagliano Bros account was justified; otherwise the bank would be required to reimburse Vagliano Bros.

The House of Lords *held* that the payee is 'fictitious' within the meaning of s 7(3) even though the name is that of an existing person, where the name has been inserted by way of pretence without any intention that he should ever receive payment. The bills being bearer bills, the forged indorsements were immaterial.

The bill is also a bearer bill if the drawer signs in favour of a person of whose existence he is unaware, the payee being deemed to be 'non-existing'.

CLUTTON v. ATTENBOROUGH & SONS [1897] AC 90

A clerk falsely represented to his employer that work had been done by Brett. The employer drew a cheque in Brett's favour even though no-one of that name was in fact known to him and that no work had been done. The clerk indorsed the cheque in the name of 'Brett' and negotiated it for value.

The House of Lords *held* that the payee was non-existent and the cheque was therefore payable to bearer. The forged indorsements were therefore irrelevant, bearer cheques being transferable by delivery without indorsement, and the current holder of the bill had a good title to it.

However, eight years later the above two cases were distinguished in the following.

VINDEN v. HUGHES [1905] 1 KB 795

A fraudulent clerk made out cheques to certain well-known customers and persuaded his employer to sign the cheques even though no money was in fact owing to those customers. The clerk then forged indorsements and negotiated the cheques for value.

It was *held* that the payees were not fictitious because the drawer believed he owed money to the payees who were known to him and he intended those payees to receive payment. The bills were not therefore payable to bearer and the drawers could recover the money wrongly debited from their account by the drawee bank.

A distinction therefore needs to be made between a fictitious person and a fictitious purpose. The latter will not constitute a bill a bearer bill.

The decision in *Vinden* v. *Hughes* was followed three years later in *North & South Wales Bank Ltd* v. *Macbeth* [1908] AC 137. The facts of this later case are very similar to those of *Vinden* v. *Hughes*.

4 The Contractual Aspects of a Bill

A bill of exchange is a contract evidencing that a debt is owed by the drawer to the payee. The debt will either be paid by the drawer himself or by the drawee. Therefore there must be consideration for the debt.

S 5(2) provides that where the drawer and the drawee are the same person, or the drawee is a fictitious person or a person not having capacity to contract, the holder may treat the instrument at his option as either a promissory note or a bill of exchange (see Chapter 3).

Where the drawer and the drawee are separate persons there is normally an obligation or debt existing between them, thus providing a reason why the drawee should transfer money to the payee at the order of the drawer.

CAPACITY TO CONTRACT

S 22 provides that capacity to incur liability as a party to the bill is co-extensive with the capacity to contract. Where a bill is drawn or indorsed by a minor or corporation having no capacity or power to incur liability on a bill, the drawing or indorsement entitles the holder to receive payment on the bill and to enforce it against any other party liable on the bill. The minor, for instance, is never liable *on the bill*, not even if it is accepted or given by him in return for necessaries (*Re Soltykoff, Ex parte Margrett* [1891] 1 QB 413), and not even if it is post-dated to a date after he attains his eighteenth birthday. On the other hand, the holder will be entitled to receive payment of the bill against any party to it other than the minor or corporation without capacity, as the case may be.

> Thus if Able, a minor, draws a cheque on the Brown Bank in favour of Cain, a shopkeeper, who has supplied him with necessaries and Cain, the payee, indorses a cheque to Mark, the cheque is dishonoured. Mark will be unable to sue Able, the minor, but can sue Cain on his indorsement. It should be noted that although Cain, too, is unable to sue Able *on the cheque* he can claim a reasonable price for the necessaries sold and delivered under s 2, Sale of Goods Act, 1979.

Regarding corporations, if they are trading companies there is an implied power to draw, accept and indorse bills of exchange, and since the practice

23

of drawing cheques is universal, the implied power probably extends to non-trading companies as well.

CONSIDERATION

S 27 provides that valuable consideration for a bill may be constituted by:

(a) Any consideration sufficient to support a simple contract:
or
(b) Any antecedent debt or liability.

The antecedent debt is deemed to be valuable consideration whether the bill is payable on demand or at a future time.

It will be recalled that at common law consideration is a vital element of a valid binding contract: that consideration must be something of value but need not be adequate; and that past consideration is no consideration.

Bills are frequently drawn or accepted in settlement of past debts. Thus bills of exchange were recognised as an exception to this sacred common law principle.

Past consideration in the form of an existing debt or liability incurred as a result of an event which has already taken place is valuable consideration for a bill of exchange provided that the debt is owed by the payer to the payee.

OLIVER v. DAVIS & WOODCOCK [1949] 2 All E.R. 353

Davis owed money to Oliver. Woodcock drew a cheque naming Oliver as the payee in order to pay off Davis's debt. Woodcock later stopped the cheque. The court *held* that there was no antecedent debt owing by Woodcock to Oliver (only that owing by Davis to Oliver), and, as there was no evidence that Oliver had agreed not to sue Davis when taking the cheque from Woodcock (forbearance to sue being valuable consideration), there was no consideration for the cheque.

We can illustrate the validity of past consideration thus:

If Cain has delivered goods to Able to the value of £800 then a cheque drawn by Able to pay Cain £800 in consideration of the goods he has already acquired is a valid transaction notwithstanding that the goods have already been delivered and therefore the consideration is past.

As with other contracts, the consideration for a bill of exchange need not be adequate, although some value must be given. Thus an auctioneer's warranty that he was entitled to accept cheques for the price was held to be valuable consideration for a cheque for £555 (*Pollway* v. *Abdullah*, [1974] 2 All E.R. 381).

24

HOLDERS AND THEIR RIGHTS

The Act prescribes that a person may be in possession of a bill as:

(1) Holder in due course, or

(2) Holder for value, or

(3) Holder.

(1) Holder in due course

In order for the holder of a bill to overcome a defect on a bill, thus enjoying the major attribute of negotiability, he must show either that he is a holder in due course or that, at least, he has taken the bill through a holder in due course (s 29(3)). Thus:

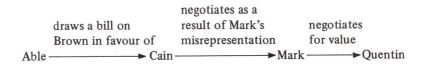

If Quentin can satisfy the definition of holder in due course the defect is cured, and he will be entitled to sue the other parties to the bill. Furthermore, if Quentin does satisfy the definition and then negotiates the bill to Xavier, the result of s 29(3) (see page 28) is that it is immaterial whether or not Xavier is a holder in due course, and so long as he is not a party to any fraud he can enforce the bill against any person whom Mark could have sued.

A holder in due course is defined as a holder who has taken a bill complete and regular on the face provided (s 29(1)) (a) he became holder of it before it was overdue and without notice that it had previously been dishonoured, if such was the fact, and (b) that he took the bill in good faith and for value, and that at the time the bill was negotiated to him he had no notice of any defect in title of the person who negotiated it to him.

Such is the importance of this definition that we will analyse it.

(a) **Holder.** Although the definition of 'holder' includes the payee, the House of Lords *held* in *Jones* v. *Waring and Gillow Ltd* [1926] A.C. 670 that the original payee has the bill *issued* to him, not *negotiated* to him as required by s 29(1).

25

Therefore if as a result of Mrs Cain's fraud Able is induced to draw a cheque in favour of Cain, Able will have a defence to Cain's claim on the cheque despite Cain's innocence. (Of course, if Cain indorses the cheque to Mark who, in all respects, satisfies the definition of a holder in due course, the position would be otherwise.)

(b) Complete and regular on the face of it. For example, the bill must not contain an uninitialled alteration, nor must there be a serious discrepancy between the payee's name on the front of the bill and his indorsement on the back.

(c) Before it was overdue. A demand bill is overdue which has been circulating for an unreasonable time; a time bill is overdue when the due date for payment has passed.

(d) Good faith. By s 90 a thing is deemed to be done in good faith where it is, in fact, done honestly, whether it is done negligently or not.

(e) For value. The value (even if it is past consideration) must have been given by the holder himself.

(f) Without notice of defect. This means either actual notice of some fraud or illegality, or a wilful disregard of the means of knowledge in suspicious circumstances.

It is the holder in due course who acquires all the benefits of negotiation. These benefits are particularly apparent when negotiation of bills of exchange is compared with the assignment of contracts:

(i) The holder in due course of a bill takes free from defects in title; the assignee of a contract takes the contract subject to defect in title whether or not he has previous notice of them.

(ii) Neither the drawer nor the drawee need be given notice of a transfer of title of a bill for a negotiation to be valid; whenever a contract is assigned notice must be given to the debtor (s 136, Law of Property Act, 1925).

Negotiation is practically easier to operate than assignment and reflects the commercial necessity for an instrument in which a sum ordered to be paid will be paid to the rightful holder of the bill.

S 29(2) provides that the title of a person who negotiates a bill is defective when he obtained the bill or the acceptance of a bill by:

(i) Fraud, or

26

(ii) Duress, or

(iii) Force and fear, or

(iv) Other unlawful means, or

(v) An illegal consideration, or

(vi) Negotiation in breach of faith, or

(vii) Circumstances which amount to fraud.

Where a person acquires a bill in any of these circumstances he cannot be a holder in due course.

(2) Holder for value

A holder for value is someone who is in possession of a bill for which value has at some time been given. The value may be given by himself or some previous party to the bill. S 27(2) provides that where value has at any time been given for a bill the holder is deemed to be a holder for value as regards the acceptor and all parties to the bill who became parties prior to that time: in other words, consideration need not move from the promisee, and a person seeking to enforce the bill need not himself have given consideration. Thus:

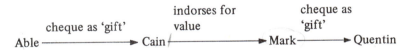

If the cheque is dishonoured, Quentin can sue both Able and Cain, being parties prior to the time that value was last given; but he cannot sue Mark, the absence of consideration between immediate parties being a defence.

In the case of *Diamond* v. *Graham* [1968] 2 All E.R. 909 the Court of Appeal *held* that it is not essential to the operation of s 27(2) that the person giving value for the bill (Mark) is a party to the bill.

Once consideration has been given for a bill all subsequent holders will be holders for value. But where there is a 'defect' on a bill it is not enough for a holder to be a holder for value. Unlike the holder in due course, the holder for value takes the bill subject to 'equities', and can be met with defences of fraud, duress or illegality by parties to the bill at or before the time of the fraud.

When the holder of a bill has a lien on that bill he is deemed to be a holder

27

for value to the extent of that lien (s 27(3)). Thus:

> If Cain is given a cheque for £200 which he asks his bank to collect at a time when he has an overdraft of £150, the bank has a lien on that £200 cheque to the extent of £150. Similarly, if Cain, the holder of the bill for £200, deposits the bill with his bank as security for the £150 overdraft, the bank is a holder for value as to £150, and could recover this amount in an action against Cain or other parties.

S 30(1) provides a presumption that every party whose signature appears on a bill is *prima facie* deemed to have become a party to the bill for value. Therefore, in contrast to ordinary contracts, consideration is presumed to have been given for a bill of exchange. Furthermore, every holder of a bill is *prima facie* deemed to be a holder in due course. The holder will only have to prove that value has, in good faith, been given if it is proved that the issue, acceptance or negotiation of a bill is affected with fraud, duress or illegality (s 30 (2)).

(3) Holder

A 'holder' is the term given to the person currently in possession of the bill, being either the payee or indorsee of an order bill who is in possession, or the bearer of a bearer bill. A person holding a forgery or one who has stolen a bill payable to order is not a holder but a wrongful possessor, but a thief would be the 'holder' of a bearer bill.

S 29(3) provides that a holder (whether for value or not) who derives his title to a bill through a holder in due course and who is not himself a party to any fraud or illegality affecting the bill has all the rights of a holder in due course as regards the acceptor and all the parties to the bill prior to that holder.

> Using a similar example, if Cain, as the original payee and holder of the bill, negotiates the bill to Mark for value, then, provided that Mark becomes the holder of the bill:
>
> (i)   before it is overdue,
>
> (ii) without notice that it has previously been dishonoured,
>
> (iii) that he takes the bill in good faith, and
>
> (iv) that at the time of negotiation he has no notice of any defect in title on the part of Cain, then Mark is the holder in due course of the bill.

28

If Mark then negotiates but gives the bill to Quentin, in other words, Mark receives no consideration or value from Quentin in return for the receipt of the bill, then Quentin is not a holder in due course: Quentin is merely a holder for value. However, Quentin has all the rights of Mark against prior parties.

SIGNATURE

S 23 provides that no person is liable as drawer, indorser or acceptor of a bill who has not signed it as such. Thus:

> Brown, the drawee of our bill, will not be liable on it until he has 'accepted' (signed) it, and the bank on whom a cheque is drawn will not be liable to the holder if payment is refused.

Once any of these parties has added his signature to the bill he is liable to pay the sum stated in the bill to the rightful holder on the day of maturity; in other words, on the day the payment falls due. Where a person signs a bill otherwise than as drawee or acceptor he incurs the liability of an indorser to the holder in due course (s 56). Thus a director of a company may sign the back of a bill drawn upon his company to secure a loan to the company by a third party; the director 'backs' the bill and will be liable as indorser to a holder in due course.

If a person signs a bill in the mistaken belief that he is signing a different type of document, he may be able to avoid liability by pleading *non est factum* (it was not my deed), although this defence will be lost unless he can show that he was not careless when signing the document.

It is not necessary that a party signs with his own hand: it is sufficient that his signature is written on the bill by some other person by or under his authority (s 91). Under s 33, Companies Act, 1948, a company will be liable as a party to a bill if the bill is made, accepted or indorsed in the name of or by and on behalf or on account of the company by any persons acting under its authority. The company's name must be written legibly and the word 'limited' or 'ltd' (in the case of a limited company) must also be shown, otherwise the officer responsible for the attaching of the signature will be personally liable to the holder of the instrument, unless it is paid by the company itself (Companies Act, 1948, s 108(4)).

Where a person signs a bill in a trade name or assumed name he is liable on the bill as if he had signed it in his own name.

The signature of the name of a firm (partnership) is equivalent to the signature by the person signing the names of all persons liable as partners in that firm. The liability of the other partners will depend upon whether the party signing had express or implied authority to bind them, although, in the case of a trading firm, it is conclusively presumed in favour of a holder in due course that the other partners are bound.

A signature by procuration usually evidenced by the abbreviation 'per pro' operates as notice that the agent has but a limited authority to sign, and the principal is only bound by such a signature if, in so signing, the agent was acting within the actual limits of his authority. A third party cannot rely on the agency doctrine of 'apparent or ostensible' authority where an agent signs a bill of exchange 'per pro'. If the bill is for an amount in excess of the agent's actual authority the principal will only be liable to the third party to the extent of the actual authority.

MORISON v. KEMP (1912) 29 TLR 70

A clerk employed by a firm of insurance brokers who was authorised to sign cheques 'per pro' his employers for the purposes of their business drew a cheque in this form in favour of his bookmaker to settle his private betting losses: the bookmaker cashed the cheque. It was *held* that the employers could recover the amount of the cheque from the bookmaker.

Where a person signs a bill as drawer, indorser or acceptor and adds words to his signature indicating that he signs for or on behalf of his principal, or in a representative capacity, he is not personally liable on the bill. If a person merely adds to his signature words which describe him as an agent or a person filling a representative role he is not exempted from personal liability. This will be a question of fact in every case. Thus a cheque signed 'A. Able, director' will render Able personally liable, but not a signature 'A. Able, director Greenbrook Products Ltd'.

In determining whether a signature on a bill is that of the principal or that of the agent by whose hand it is written, the construction most favourable to the validity of the instrument is the one adopted (s 26(2)).

ELLIOTT v. BAX-IRONSIDE (1925) 2 KB 301

A bill was addressed to the Fashion Fair Exhibition Company Ltd. It was accepted 'AB: CD: directors, Fashion Fair Exhibition Co. Ltd' and indorsed in the same manner. The bill was *held* to be validly accepted by the company but indorsed personally by the directors. It was favourable to the validity of the bill that the indorsement be regarded as the personal indorsement of the directors, the company being liable anyway to the holder as acceptor.

FORGED AND UNAUTHORISED SIGNATURES

When a signature on a bill is forged or unauthorised the signature is wholly inoperative. Once a forged or unauthorised signature has been written on a bill, s 24 states that 'no right to retain the bill or to give a discharge therefore or to enforce payment thereof against any party thereto can be acquired through or under that signature'.

The person responsible for the forgery is not entitled to payment of the amount stated in the bill, and the forger in negotiating the bill can only pass on the title which he has to the bill. A forger cannot pass on a good title to the bill. A forger does not benefit from the concept of negotiation. A forged signature is no signature at all, and cannot pass any title to the bill. A forged signature can never be overcome.

An unauthorised signature is one placed on the bill without the authority of the person whose signature it purports to be. Such a signature, unlike a forged signature, may be ratified. In the event of ratification the signature is retrospectively valid, and the party responsible for the signature is liable on the bill. Thus where a clerk employed by Cain Ltd, a company, without authority indorses bills payable to Cain Ltd to the company's creditors, then the creditors' lack of title to the bills could be made good if Cain Ltd ratified the indorsement. Taking our example again:

(1) If Able's, the drawer's signature is forged or is written without his authority then he will not be liable as drawer of the bill: indeed the instrument, not being 'signed by the person giving it' within the meaning of s 3, is not really a bill at all, and there can be no holder of the bill. Therefore if Cain steals Able's cheque book, forges Able's signature as drawer, and cashes the cheque with Mark, Mark's only remedy will be an action against Cain: Able cannot be sued.

Contrast cases such as *Clutton* v. *Attenborough* and *Vinden* v. *Hughes* (see Chapter 3), where fraudulent clerks drew up cheques on which they obtained their employer's signature as drawer. Such a signature is neither forged nor unauthorised. The employers willingly added their signatures to the cheques.

(2) If Cain's, the payee's signature is forged. If Cain loses the bill and the person finding it, Xavier, forges Cain's signature on the reverse of the bill the bill would look as if it was payable to bearer, entitling the holder at maturity to claim payment. The forged signature of Cain is, however, wholly inoperative (s 24), and should Xavier succeed in claiming payment of the £800 from Brown, the drawee, Brown would still also be liable to Cain for the £800.

(3) If Brown's, the drawee's signature is forged. The signature of Brown will only appear on the bill if the bill has been accepted by Brown. The drawee named in a bill is not liable on the bill unless he accepts the bill. Thus the bill does not require the signature of a drawee.

By signing, Brown would make himself primarily liable on the bill to the party who is holder in due course at the date of maturity. Brown will not be liable as acceptor unless he has signed the bill as such (s 23), but Able, the drawer, and subsequent indorsers will be liable to the holder for value. If Brown's signature is forged or is placed on the bill without his authority it is wholly inoperative.

In *The Bank of England* v. *Vagliano Bros* (see Chapter 3) a fraudulent clerk obtained the signature of Vagliano Bros as a genuine acceptance of bills purported to be drawn by a customer of Vagliano Bros in favour of P & Co. The clerk then forged P & Co.'s signature. It will be recalled that because the payee named in the bill was fictitious the bill was payable to bearer: the forgery of P & Co.'s signature is therefore irrelevant. Vagliano Bros were liable to the holder in due course (the Bank of England), the signature of acceptance being genuine.

(4) If a forged indorsement is placed on a bill there can be no future holders in due course of that bill. A person who does take a bill after a forged indorsement will have a right of action against all parties subsequent to the forged indorsement, but he does not have a right against those persons who were parties to the bill prior to the forged signature. Thus:

The bill is drawn by Able upon Brown and is made payable to Cain. Cain is the payee of the bill and the person initially entitled to negotiate the bill. Considering the following events:

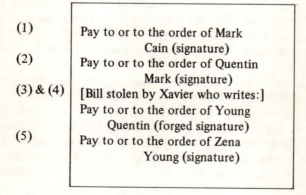

(1)   Pay to or to the order of Mark
              Cain (signature)
(2)   Pay to or to the order of Quentin
              Mark (signature)
(3) & (4)   [Bill stolen by Xavier who writes:]
           Pay to or to the order of Young
              Quentin (forged signature)
(5)   Pay to or to the order of Zena
              Young (signature)

(1) Cain negotiates the bill to Mark. Provided that Mark gives valuable consideration for the bill and that he has no notice of a defect in title on the part of Cain, Mark is the holder in due course and the person entitled to payment on the maturity of the bill.

(2) Mark negotiates the bill to Quentin. Quentin is now presumed to be the holder in due course. Mark, Cain and Able are liable to Quentin.

(3) Xavier steals the bill from Quentin and forges Quentin's indorsement to 'negotiate' the bill to Young.

(4) Young acquires no better title to the bill than that of Xavier (in fact, no title at all!); Young is not a holder in due course. Young will be able to sue Xavier for the amount stated in the bill but is not entitled to payment from any party prior to the forgery, Able, Cain, Mark or Quentin. In the event of Young presenting the bill for payment to Brown, the drawee, and obtaining payment, the bill will not be discharged. Brown, if he has accepted the bill, will remain liable to Quentin, who on regaining rightful possession of the bill could make Brown pay again the amount stated in the bill. (This does not necessarily apply if the instrument is a cheque and Brown is the bank on which it is drawn, since bankers have statutory protection in the event of forged indorsements on cheques (see Chapter 10).)

However, Brown may be able to recover the amount he has paid to Young as money paid under mistake of fact so long as he takes immediate action to correct the mistake. Thus in *London and River Plate Bank* v. *Bank of Liverpool* [1896] 1 QB 7 a delay of six weeks was *held* to prevent the acceptor from recovering the money he had paid out.

(5) Young negotiates the bill to Zena. Zena, in the event of dishonour for non-payment by Brown, would have a right of action against Young but not against the parties prior to the forged signature.

A person may be estopped or precluded from pleading forgery or unauthorised signature if he has known of the forgery and has failed to notify the others within a reasonable amount of time.

GREENWOOD v. MARTINS BANK LTD [1933] AC 51

A man's wife repeatedly forged her husband's signature on cheques and drew out money from his bank account which she used for her own purposes. The husband became aware of the forgeries but kept silent for eight months. The husband then sued the bank to recover the sums his bank had paid out of his account on cheques on which his signature had been forged by his wife. The House of Lords *held* that the husband owed a duty to disclose the forgeries to his bank when he became aware of them, and, failing ·in that duty, the husband was estopped from claiming that the signatures were forgeries. He was therefore not entitled to recover the sums debited to his account.

NEGOTIATION

(1) Order bills

The ability to transfer the entitlement to a bill is one of the fundamental characteristics of a bill of exchange and is the reason for their existence and development. The proferring of a written instrument evidencing that money will be paid at a fixed future date given in exchange for goods received enabled merchants to use these written instruments, which became known as bills of exchange, to settle their debts with a third party by transferring the bill to that third party; he in turn could transfer the bill and so on until the date of payment arrived. On that date the holder of the bill could collect the money as originally prescribed by the drawer. It is the act of transferring entitlement to a bill which is known as negotiation.

S 31 provides that a bill is negotiated when it is transferred from one person to another in such a manner as to constitute the transferee the holder of the bill. A bill payable to bearer is negotiated by mere delivery, whereas a bill payable to order is negotiated by the indorsement of the holder and is completed by delivery.

Where negotiation requires an indorsement the indorsement must comply with the following rules which are found in s 32:

(a) It must be written on the bill itself and signed by the indorser. The simple signature of the indorser, like the simple signature of the acceptor, is sufficient. (A slip of paper called an allonge may be attached to the bill if there is no further space on the bill.)

(b) It must be an indorsement of the whole bill. An indorsement which purports to transfer to the indorsee only part of the amount payable or which purports to transfer the bill to two or more indorsees severally is not an operative negotiation.

(c) Where a bill is made payable to or to the order of two or more payees or indorsees who are not partners they must all indorse the bill unless one has authority to indorse for the others.

(d) Where a bill is payable to or to the order of a payee or indorsee whose name is mis-spelt or title incorrect, he may indorse as described and may add his proper signature if he thinks fit.

(e) Where there are two or more indorsements on a bill each indorsement is deemed to have been made in the order in which it appears on the bill unless the contrary is proved.

An indorsement may be made *in blank*, in which case the indorsee merely adds his signature to the bill. Such a bill then becomes a bearer bill (s 34 (1)). Alternatively, an indorsement may be *special*, as where the indorsee signs the bill and expressly states to whom or to whose order the bill is now payable (s 34(2)). However, any condition added by the indorser may be ignored by the drawee/acceptor and payment to the indorsee is valid irrespective of the condition (s 33). This provision relates to the definition of a bill of exchange, which requires an unconditional order in writing (s 3).

Whenever a bill has been indorsed in blank any holder may (for greater security) convert the blank indorsement into a special indorsement by writing above the indorser's signature a direction to pay the bill to himself or some other person (s 34(4)).

In addition the indorser may insert a statement negativing or limiting his authority to the holder and waiving as regards himself some or all of the holder's duties (s 16). A phrase commonly used by indorsers to indicate their limited responsibility to future holders of the bill is *sans recours*. Such a qualification will invariably be added by an agent who indorses on behalf of his principal.

When a bill purports to be *indorsed conditionally*, such as 'Pay Mark on his marriage to Esther' or 'Pay Xavier if he hands over the bill of lading', s 33 states that the payer *may* disregard the condition and pay Mark and Xavier whether or not the condition has been fulfilled. Alternatively, the payer may, if he wishes, refuse payment until the condition is satisfied.

A *restrictive indorsement* (as opposed to a conditional indorsement) is effective, and may prohibit further negotiation of the bill or limit the future use of the bill by, for example, indorsing the bill 'Pay D only' or 'Pay D for the account of X' (s 35). Such an indorsement gives the indorsee the right to receive payment of the bill and to sue any party that his indorser could have sued in the event of dishonour but gives him no power to transfer his rights as indorsee unless there is an express authorisation. Thus:

> Cain, the payee of a cheque, owes money to Mark, an overseas supplier, and he wishes to indorse the cheque over to George, Mark's British agent, but wants to make it absolutely clear that George is not the beneficial owner of the cheque. Cain can indorse the cheque 'Pay George for the account of Mark'. George can obtain payment and must then account to Mark; he cannot transfer the bill.

A restrictive indorsement does authorise transfer; all subsequent indorsees take the bill with the same rights and subject to the same restrictions as the first indorsee under the restrictive indorsement.

S 8(1) provides that when a bill contains words prohibiting transfer it is valid between the immediate parties but is not negotiable. Here the draftsmen presumably should have used the word 'transferable' rather than 'negotiable'. Thus a bill (including a cheque) drawn 'Pay Cain only' or marked 'not transferable', although valid between the parties, cannot be transferred at all. It was held in *Hibernian Bank Ltd* v. *Gysin and Hanson* [1939] 1 KB 483 that the words 'not negotiable' on a bill which was not a cheque rendered the bill not transferable. However, a cheque carrying the words 'not negotiable' remains transferable, but the transferee no longer enjoys the major attribute of a negotiable instrument, the enjoyment of freedom from defects in the transferor's title.

Thus the words 'not negotiable' written across the face of a bill of exchange prohibit transfer.

Where a bill is negotiable in its origin it continues to be negotiable until it has either been restrictively indorsed or discharged by payment (s 36). Where an overdue bill is negotiated it can only be negotiated subject to any defect of title affecting it at its maturity, that is, the date on which it falls due for payment. From that date onward no person can acquire or give a better title than the transferor. Unless an indorsement bears a date after maturity of the bill every negotiation is presumed to have been effected before the bill was overdue unless the contrary is proved.

The effect of indorsement is stated in s 55(2) to be that the indorser by indorsing is promising that when the bill is presented it will be accepted and paid according to the instructions written on the bill, and that if it is dishonoured he will compensate the holder or any subsequent indorser who is compelled to pay it providing the necessary proceedings on dishonour are followed: thus an indorser is liable as a surety on the bill. An indorser cannot deny to the holder in due course the genuineness and regularity of the drawer's signature and all previous indorsements. Similarly the indorser cannot deny that he has a good title to the bill neither to his immediate indorsee nor to all subsequent indorsees. Thus having signed the bill an indorser cannot plead reasons why he should not be liable to subsequent holders of the bill.

Finally, if the holder of an order bill transfers it *for value* but without indorsing it, the transference operates merely as an assignment in that the transferee takes the bill subject to equities and cannot sue on the bill in his own name; however, he does acquire a right to have the bill indorsed by the transferor. Thus:

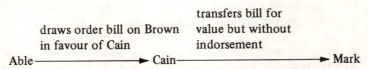

Mark will be an equitable assignee of the bill until it is indorsed and will therefore obtain no better rights to the bill than those enjoyed by Cain, unless and until he compels Cain to indorse. If Cain refuses, the court has power under s 47, Judicature Act, 1925 to order another person to sign on his behalf.

(2) Bearer bills

Where the holder of a bearer bill negotiates it by delivery without indorsing it (as, of course, he is entitled to do), he is called a 'transferor by delivery', and will not be liable on the instrument. However, if he negotiates a bill he warrants to his immediate transferee being a holder for value that the bill is what it purports to be, that he has a right to transfer it, and that at the time of transfer he is not aware of any fact that renders it valueless (s 58(2)).

Thus whilst the transferor by delivery incurs liability in respect of any breach of the stated warranties to his immediate transferee who has given value for the bill, he does not guarantee acceptance or payment of the bill and cannot be sued by transferees beyond his immediate transferee. So if it is subsequently found that the drawer's signature has been forged a transferor by delivery can be sued by his transferee, not on the bill itself, but for breach of warranty.

DELIVERY

Simple indorsement by the holder of an order bill will not operate to negotiate the bill — it must also be delivered. This follows from s 21(1), which states that every contract on a bill, whether it be the drawer's, acceptor's or an indorser's, is incomplete and revocable until delivery of the instrument. Delivery is the transfer of possession, actual or constructive (e.g. where an agent agrees to hold the bill for a different principal), from one person to another. However, once an acceptance is written on a bill and the drawee gives notice to or according to the directions of the persons entitled to the bill, the acceptance becomes complete and irrevocable even before delivery (s 21). Moreover, by s 21(3) where a bill is no longer in possession of a party who has signed as drawer, acceptor or indorser, a valid and unconditional delivery by him is presumed until the contrary is proved.

To be effectual, the delivery must be made either by or under the authority of the drawer, acceptor or indorser as the case may be; the delivery may be shown to have been conditional or for a special purpose only and not for the purpose of transferring the property in the bill. Nevertheless, if the bill be in the hands of a holder in due course a valid delivery of the bill by all parties prior to him so as to make them liable to him is conclusively presumed (s 21).

Thus if Able draws a cheque in favour of Cain or order and Cain indorses it in blank, converting it into a bearer cheque, and a thief steals the cheque from Cain, the thief has no title because there was no delivery to him. But if the thief then negotiates the cheque to Mark, a holder in due course, Mark can sue all prior parties because in his case delivery from Cain to the thief is conclusively presumed.

INCHOATE INSTRUMENTS

S 20(1) provides that where a simple signature on a blank paper is delivered by the signer in order that it may be converted into a bill it operates as an authority to fill it as a complete bill for any amount using the signature for that of either (i) the drawer, (ii) the acceptor, or (iii) the indorser.

Similarly, when a bill is wanting in any material particular the person in possession of it has authority to fill up the omission in any way he thinks fit. Thus:

> If Able owes Cain £500 and writes an acceptance for that amount on a piece of paper and hands it to Cain, Cain can write in his own name as drawer and payee and sue Able on the bill.

The above provisions, however, only apply *prima facie*, and therefore may be challenged at least until the bill as completed comes into the hands of a holder in due course.

For an inchoate instrument to be enforceable against a person who becomes a party prior to the completion of the bill it must be filled in (a) within a reasonable time (this is always a question of fact which depends on the circumstances) and (b) strictly in accordance with the authority given (s 20(2)).

Inchoate means incomplete, and s 20 gives, basically, authority to create a bill of exchange. Inchoate bills are commonly found in the form of blank cheques. Delivery of the inchoate bill operates as authority to fill up the bill and so complete it. Thus:

> If Able signs a piece of paper but does not complete it as a bill and delivers it to Cain as payment for a filing cabinet then Able will be liable on the bill as completed by Cain provided that Cain did so complete within a reasonable time and according to Able's instructions.

If the person to whom the inchoate bill was delivered completes the bill for an amount greater than he is authorised by the drawer, the drawer will not be liable to the person so completing. But if or when such a bill comes into the hands of a holder in due course who has no knowledge that it has been filled in contrary to the drawer's instructions, the drawer will nevertheless be liable to the holder in due course for the amount stated on the bill. Thus:

> If Able authorises Cain to complete the bill for the amount of the price of the filing cabinet and Cain fills in the bill for a greater amount, Able is not liable to Cain for that greater amount. If, however, the bill, so completed, comes into the hands of Mark, who satisfies the definitions of a holder in due course, Able is liable to Mark for the amount as stated on the bill.

Although the original payee can never be a holder in due course because the bill is not negotiated to him, he may, with respect to inchoate bills, be able to rely on the doctrine of estoppel, and so claim the amount stated in the bill from the drawer albeit in excess of the amount authorised to be stated in the bill by the drawer.

LLOYDS BANK LTD v. COOKE [1907] 1 KB 974

The defendant signed his name on a blank piece of paper and handed it to a customer of the plaintiffs with authority to fill it up as a promissory note for a specified sum payable to the plaintiff and to deliver the note to the plaintiffs as security for an advance. The customer filled in a larger amount and obtained that amount from the plaintiffs. The court *held* that the defendant was estopped from denying the validity of the note as between himself and the plaintiffs. The plaintiffs were not a holder in due course because they were the original payee. Nevertheless, in the circumstances the drawer was liable for the amount stated in the note, albeit in excess of the amount he had authorised by virtue of the doctrine of estoppel.

5 Acceptance, Payment and Dishonour

ACCEPTANCE

Recalling that there are basically three parties to a bill of exchange, the drawer, the drawee and the payee, acceptance is the procedure by which the drawee acknowledges the order stated in the bill and undertakes to pay the payee or any subsequent indorser the amount stated in the bill as directed by the drawer. S 17(1) defines acceptance as the 'signification by the drawee of his assent to the order of the drawer'. The drawee makes himself liable by the act of signing the bill (s 23). The acceptance is not, however, complete until either the bill has been delivered by, or under the authority of, the acceptor, or the acceptor, having accepted in writing, gives notice to the person entitled that he has accepted it. In either event the acceptance then becomes complete and irrevocable (s 21(1)). Thus:

> Able is the drawer, Brown the drawee and Cain the payee. If the bill is presented to Brown by Cain, or any subsequent holder of the bill for acceptance, the signature of Brown on the bill will render Brown the acceptor and thenceforth primarily liable to pay the sum stated in the bill when it falls due for payment.

A bill may be presented for acceptance by any holder of the bill, and s 18 provides that the bill may even be presented:

(1) Before it has been signed by the drawer or is otherwise incomplete.

(2) When it is overdue or has been dishonoured by a previous non-acceptance or non-payment.

The drawee accepts the bill by signing it and commonly by writing or stamping across the face of the bill the word 'Accepted'. Thus the drawee becomes the acceptor of the bill. S 17(2) states that the mere signature of the drawee is sufficient but that acceptance is only valid if the drawee undertakes to perform his promise by payment of money and by no other means.

If the drawee fails or refuses to accept the bill it is said to be dishonoured for non-acceptance, and in that event all the indorsers and the drawer are

40

immediately liable to pay the present holder who does not have to wait for the bill to mature. (Presentment for payment is not necessary.) The liability of the drawer and indorsers will, however, be extinguished if they do not receive notice of dishonour as required by s 48 (see page 46).

(1) Presentment for acceptance

Acceptance is not always an essential procedure (for instance, if the bill is payable on demand a holder can present the bill to the drawee at any time for actual *payment*) but it is nevertheless an advisable step to take. A bill is regarded with more favour when the person indicated as drawee has undertaken to carry out the order of the drawer and pay the amount stated to the payee or any subsequent indorser if the bill has been negotiated.

By s 39 a bill must be presented for acceptance if: (1) it is drawn payable after sight (in order to fix the maturity of the instrument); (2) it is drawn payable at a place other than the drawee's place of residence or business; (3) it expressly states that presentment for acceptance shall be made.

Where a bill is expressed to be payable X days after sight, the relevant sight is the sighting of the bill by the drawee. Acceptance therefore determines the maturity of such bills. Sight bills must, however, be presented for acceptance within a reasonable time (s 40), otherwise the previous indorsers and drawer are discharged from their liabilities. What is reasonable will depend upon the nature of the bill, the custom with respect to similar bills, and the facts of the particular case. Where a bill payable after sight is dishonoured for non-acceptance but is subsequently accepted by the drawee, the holder of the bill is entitled to have the acceptance dated as at the time of the previous presentment (s 18(3)). This backdating procedure is important, because the time for payment stated in the bill will run from the first presentment for acceptance and not the actual date of acceptance.

If a bill expressed to be payable X days after sight has been presented for acceptance and the acceptance is undated, any holder may insert the true date of acceptance and the bill shall be payable accordingly. If, however, the wrong date is inserted by the holder in good faith and by mistake and the bill subsequently comes into the hands of a holder in due course the bill is not thereby avoided but operates and is payable as if the date so inserted were the true date (s 12).

The bill must be presented for acceptance personally or by post, if this has been agreed or is the custom. The presentment must be at a reasonable hour on a business day to the drawee or to some other person authorised to act on his behalf and before the bill is overdue (s 41(1)). If a bill is accepted when it is overdue with respect to the acceptor the bill is deemed to be payable on demand (s 10(2)).

Presentment must be made to all the drawees where a bill is addressed to two or more drawees unless they are partners or one has authority to accept

41

for all. Where the drawee is dead presentment *may* be made to his personal representative or if bankrupt to his trustee in bankruptcy. Where authorised by agreement or usage a presentment through the post is sufficient (s 41(2)).

If a person signs a bill as acceptor and indicates that he is signing on behalf of a principal he is not personally liable thereon, but the mere addition to his signature of the word 'agent' does not exempt him from personal liability.

Presentment is excused (s 41(2)) and a bill may be treated as dishonoured for non-acceptance where the drawee is dead, bankrupt, a fictitious person, a person with no capacity to contract or where, after the exercise of reasonable diligence, acceptance cannot be effected. Where a bill is required to be accepted presentment is not excused if the holder believes that the bill will be dishonoured for non-acceptance: the holder must nevertheless present (s 41 (3)).

(2) Types of acceptance

Acceptance may be either general or qualified. General acceptance is the drawee's unconditional assent to the drawer's order evidenced by his signature and usually the word 'Accepted'. The drawee thereby agrees to carry out the order of the drawer (s 19(2)). Qualified acceptance varies the effect of the bill as drawn; the drawee attaches conditions to his paying the sum ordered by the drawer. Payment may be made conditional upon:

(a) Some event: for instance, upon delivery of a consignment of goods or 'on delivery of bills of lading'.

(b) Payment being made at a certain place and only at that place, e.g. 'accepted payable at Lloyds Bank Mudville only'. If, however, a place is indicated as a possible place of payment the acceptance may be treated as general: this will be so if the word 'only' was omitted from the above acceptance.

(c) The expiration of a certain period of time, e.g. 'accepted payable 3 months after date' written across a bill drawn payable two months after date.

Where any of these conditions are required by the drawee the holder may treat the bill as dishonoured for non-acceptance (s 44). The holder has an immediate right of recourse against the drawer and previous indorsers in such circumstances and presentment for payment is not necessary (s 43(2)).

Should the holder decide to accept any of these qualifications without first obtaining the consent of the drawer and previous indorsers, the drawer and previous indorsers are discharged from liability. If the drawer or any indorser, having received notice of a qualified acceptance, does not express his dissent within a reasonable time he shall be deemed to have consented to the qualification (s 44).

If the drawee qualifies his acceptance by providing that he will accept a bill drawn for £1,000 for £800 only, thus accepting only part of the amount ordered to be paid by the drawer, the holder can take such 'partial' acceptance and will not lose his right to sue the drawer and all previous indorsers provided he gives notice of his action to the drawer and all previous indorsers. They will remain liable in full whether they consent or not.

Thus Able draws a £1,000 bill on Brown payable to Cain, six months after date, and Cain indorses it to Mark. When Mark presents the bill to Brown for acceptance, Brown accepts 'as to £800 only'. Mark can, of course, refuse this and serve notice of dishonour and take proceedings against the drawer, Able, and against the indorser Cain. On the other hand, Mark may take the partial acceptance, in which case on notifying Able and Cain he can hold them liable immediately for the £200 for which the bill has been dishonoured. Of course, if, on maturity, the £800 is not paid by Brown then they will be liable to Mark in that amount also.

(3) Effect of acceptance

S 54 provides that, by accepting, the acceptor engages that he will pay the bill according to his acceptance and that he cannot deny to the holder in due course: (a) the existence of the drawer, the genuineness of his signature nor his capacity and authority to draw the bill; (b) in the case of a bill payable to the drawer's order the then capacity of the drawer to indorse, but not the genuineness or validity of his indorsement; (c) in the case of a bill payable to the order of a third person, the existence of the payee and his then capacity to indorse, but not the genuineness or validity of his indorsement (s 54(2)).

If the drawee wishes to challenge any of these facts he should not accept the bill, for by accepting the drawee makes himself primarily liable on the bill; prior to this event it is the drawer who is primarily liable. Thus:

Able has apparently drawn a 'bill' on Brown in favour of Cain; the bill is accepted by Brown, but in fact Cain has forged Able's signature as drawer. If Cain negotiates the 'bill' to Mark, a holder in due course, then Mark can sue Brown because s 54(2) prevents Brown from setting up the forgery.

(4) Acceptance by other persons – accommodation bills

A person may sign a bill without receiving value simply to lend someone his name. Such a person is known as an accommodation party, and such a person may sign as drawer, indorser or acceptor. By s 28 the accommodation party will be liable to the holder for value, and it is irrelevant whether the holder knew he was an accommodation party and knew of the lack of consideration received by that party.

Thus if Brown, before he accepts the bill, realises that he is temporarily short of cash, he could approach his wealthy friend Willing. If Willing signs the bill as acceptor to accommodate Brown and help him out of his financial predicament Cain or any subsequent holder of the bill for value could sue Willing for the amount stated to be payable in the bill if, when the bill falls due for payment, it is dishonoured for non-payment, even if the holder knew that Willing gives an accommodation party. If the accommodation party, as in this example, signs a bill in the role of acceptor rather than as drawer or indorser, the instrument is known as an 'accommodation bill'.

PAYMENT

Apart from presenting the bill for acceptance the holder is under a duty to present the bill for payment. It follows therefore that the drawee may 'dishonour' the bill with respect to two stages of a bill of exchange. First, a bill may be dishonoured for non-acceptance, in which event the indorsers and drawer are immediately liable to pay the present holder; the Act does not require that such a bill must also be presented for payment. Secondly, a bill may be dishonoured for non-payment. It should be remembered that not all bills of exchange need to be presented for acceptance, and thus presentment for payment might be the drawee's first dealing with the bill. Should payment not be obtained the fact that presentment for payment was made on the due date retains for the holder the right of recourse to the drawer and indorsers.

(1) Rules as to presentment for payment

By s 45(3) presentment for payment must be made by the holder or some other person authorised to receive payment on his behalf and must be made at a reasonable hour on a business day. Presentment must be made either to the person indicated as payer (the drawee/acceptor) or to some other person authorised to pay or refuse payment on his behalf. The holder must be able to find the payer with the exercise of reasonable diligence.

A bill is presented at the proper place where the place is specified in the bill and the bill is presented there on the relevant day. Where no place is specified but the address of the drawee or acceptor is given in the bill, the bill must be presented at that address. Where no place is specified and no address is given, the bill must be presented at the drawee/acceptor's place of business if known and, if not, his ordinary residence. In any other case the bill can be presented where it is known that the drawee/acceptor can be found or at his last known place of residence or business (s 45(4)).

Where a bill has been presented at the proper place and after the exercise of reasonable diligence no person authorised to pay or refuse payment can be found, no further presentment is required to the acceptor or drawee (s 45(5)), and the bill may be treated as dishonoured for non-payment, the drawer and indorsers (though not the acceptor) being discharged.

(2) Time of presentment for payment

(a) A bill not payable on demand (a 'time bill') must be presented for payment by the holder on the day it falls due (s 45(1)). The bill falls due on the last day of the period or, if this is a non-business day, on the first business day thereafter, otherwise the drawer and indorsers (though not the acceptor who remains liable for the six-year limitation period) are discharged from liability. The rules are very strict.

YEOMAN CREDIT LTD v. GREGORY [1963] 1 WLR 343

The plaintiff finance company held a bill duly accepted 'payable at the N.P. Bank' due on 9 December. The bill had been personally indorsed by Gregory (as arranged by way of guarantee), who was managing director of the accepting company. The holders were told by another director shortly before the time for presentment that there were no funds at the N.P. Bank and that the bill should be presented at the M Bank. On the due date the bill was duly presented at the M Bank for payment without obtaining the consent of Gregory or of other indorsers. M Bank refused payment. On the following day, 10 December, it was presented to the N.P. Bank when it was again dishonoured. It was *held* that Gregory was discharged under s 45(1) since the bill should have been presented to the N.P. Bank on 9 December.

(b) A bill payable on demand must be presented for payment within a reasonable time of its issue in order to render the drawer liable, and within a reasonable time of its indorsement in order to render the indorser liable (s 45 (2)). (This provision is modified by s 74 in the case of a drawer of a cheque: see page 60.)

It is worth repeating the point that by s 52(1), where the drawee has given a general acceptance to a bill, presentment for payment is not necessary in order to render *him* liable — liability for the six-year limitation period follows as a result of his acceptance.

(3) Excuses for delay or non-presentment for payment

By s 46 delay in presenting will be excused if caused by circumstances beyond the control of the holder and not caused by his own misconduct, default, or negligence. When the cause for delay ceases, presentment must be made with reasonable diligence.

Presentment for payment is dispensed with where, after reasonable diligence, presentment cannot be effected, e.g. due to the outbreak of war. The fact that the holder has reason to believe that the bill will, on presentment, be dishonoured does not dispense with the necessity for presentment.

Presentment is also dispensed with:

(a)   Where the drawee is a fictitious person.

(b)   As regards the drawer where the drawer of the bill has no reason to believe that the bill would be paid if presented to the drawee, the drawee having no reason to be bound by the bill, e.g. where the drawee has accepted for the drawer's accommodation. Thus failure to present for payment would not deprive the holder of his right of recourse against the drawer, but it would still discharge the indorsers. Therefore to retain liability of the other parties to the bill presentment for payment should be made on the due date.

(c)   As regards an indorser where the bill has been accepted or made for the accommodation of an indorser who does not expect that the bill would be paid if presented.

(d)   Where presentment is expressly or impliedly waived.

(4) Dishonour by non-payment

S 47 provides that a bill is dishonoured for non-payment when it is presented for payment and payment is refused or cannot be obtained, or when presentment is excused and the bill is overdue and unpaid. When a bill is dishonoured for non-payment the holder has an immediate right of action against the drawer and indorser. Notice of dishonour must, however, be given to the drawer and indorsers, otherwise their liability is discharged. Similar consequences follow where there has been dishonour for non-acceptance (s 48).

NOTICE OF DISHONOUR

Once again, s 48 provides that when a bill has been dishonoured by non-acceptance or by non-payment, notice of dishonour must be given to the drawer and each indorser, and any drawer or indorser to whom such notice is not given is discharged.

This section goes on to state that if a bill is dishonoured for non-acceptance and notice is not given (to the drawer and all previous indorsers) the rights of the subsequent holders in due course will not, however, be affected. Where a

46

bill is dishonoured for non-acceptance and notice of dishonour is given it is not then necessary to give subsequent notice of dishonour for non-payment unless the bill has in the meantime been accepted and is now dishonoured for non-payment. Thus:

> Able draws a bill on Brown payable to Cain; Cain then indorses the bill to Mark who presents the bill to Brown for acceptance: Brown dishonours the bill by non-acceptance. Mark must give notice of dishonour to Cain and to Able if he wishes to render them liable and they will be discharged if Mark fails to do so. But if Mark subsequently negotiates the bill to Quentin, a holder in due course, *Quentin's* rights against Cain and Able will not be prejudiced by Mark's failure to given them notice of dishonour.

Where a bill is not overdue and is dishonoured any person who takes with notice of the dishonour takes subject to any defect in title at the time of dishonour. This does not, however, affect the rights of a holder in due course (s 36(5)) who, in order to acquire that status, must take a bill without notice of previous defects. Thus in the above example Quentin must be unaware of the dishonour when he takes the bill. Moreover, if the bill had been dishonoured by non-*payment* instead of non-acceptance Quentin could not be a holder in due course because the bill must have been overdue at the time of negotiation.

S 49 prescribes the rules which ensure that notice of dishonour is valid, and these rules are set out under headings (1) – (6):

(1) Who may give notice

(a) The notice must be given by or on behalf of the holder or by or on behalf of the indorser who is liable on the bill at the time of giving notice. Thus in the event of dishonour if the holder gives notice only to the person who negotiated the bill to him, that indorser thereby becomes liable and is able to give notice to all or any previous indorsers and to the drawer of the bill.

(b) The notice may be given by an agent and may be in his own name or in the name of the party entitled to give notice.

(2) The effect of giving notice

(a) Where notice is given by or on behalf of the holder it exists for the benefit of all subsequent holders and all prior indorsers who have a right of recourse against the party to whom it is given.

(b) Where notice is given by or on behalf of the indorser it exists for the benefit of the holder and all indorsers subsequent to the party to whom notice is given.

Thus, as a result of s 49(3)

```
        draws
        bill on          in favour
        Brown            of Cain       indorses        indorses        indorses
Able ──────────▶ Brown──────▶ Cain ──────────▶ Mark ──────────▶ Quentin──────▶ Xavier
```

In this example if Xavier, the holder, notifies Cain, the payee, of the dishonour of the bill by Brown then that notice will retain Cain's liability not just to Xavier but also to Mark and Quentin. But if Xavier wishes to retain the liability of Mark and Quentin he will have to give them notice.

Using, now, s 49(4), if Mark gives notice of dishonour to Cain, then Cain will be liable to *all* parties subsequent to him, i.e. to Quentin and Xavier as well as to Mark.

(3) Form of the notice

(a) The notice may be given in writing or by personal communication and must adequately identify the bill indicating that it has been dishonoured by non-acceptance or non-payment.

(b) The return of the dishonoured bill to the indorser or drawer is deemed to be sufficent notice of dishonour.

(c) A written notice need not be signed and may be supplemented by verbal statements.

(d) A misdescription of the bill is not fatal provided the person to whom notice is given is not misled by the inaccurate description.

(4) The recipient of the notice

(a) Notice may be given to the party entitled to receive notice or his agent.

(b) Where the drawer or indorser is dead and the person giving notice knows of the death, notice must be given to the personal representative provided he can be found with reasonable diligence.

(c) Where the drawer or indorser is bankrupt notice may be served upon him or his trustee.

(d) Where there are two or more drawers or indorsers who are not partners, notice must be given to each of them unless one has authority to receive notice for the others.

(5) When must notice be given

(a) Notice may be given as soon as the bill is dishonoured and must be given within a reasonable time. Reasonableness depends upon the circumstances:

(i) where the persons giving and receiving notice reside in the same place it is only reasonable to give or send notice to arrive no later than the day following dishonour of the bill.

HAMILTON FINANCE v. COVERLEY WESTRAY & OTHERS (1969) 1 Lloyds Rep. 53

It was *held* that the West End and City of London were the 'same place' for the purpose of this provision. The opinion was also stated that the two parties resided 'at the same place' if it was reasonable in all the circumstances to deliver the notice by hand instead of relying on the post.

(ii) Where the person giving and the person to receive reside in different places it is deemed to be reasonable if the notice is sent off the day following dishonour and, if no post on that day at a convenient hour, the day following when there is such a post.

EAGLEHILL LTD v. NEEDHAM BUILDERS LTD [1973] AC 992

The House of Lords had to decide whether a notice of dishonour for non-payment sent the day before the bill matured was valid. Viscount Dilhorne was of the opinion that: 'If a person gives notice of dishonour not knowing whether in fact the bill has been dishonoured he runs the risk that the notice is bad if it precedes the dishonour. But if in fact the bill has been dishonoured when the notice is given then the notice is true and cannot be impugned.' On the facts of the case he concluded that notice of dishonour was received to all intents and purposes as soon as and not before the bill was dishonoured, which suffices to make the notice a good notice within the meaning of the Act. The court emphasised that the holder would lose his rights if notice of dishonour were received before the bill had been dishonoured.

(b) Where a bill is dishonoured in the hands of an agent he may himself give notice to the parties liable or he may give notice to his principal. If an agent elects to give notice to his principal he must do so within the same period as indicated in (a) above as if he were an independent holder.

(c) Where a party receives due notice of dishonour he has the same time period as indicated in (a) above after receipt of a notice of dishonour for giving notice to antecedent parties as the holder has after dishonour. Thus:

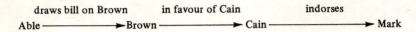

If all parties reside in the 'same place' and Brown dishonours by non-acceptance on 1 April and Mark serves notice of dishonour upon Cain which reaches him on 2 April, Cain now has further 24 hours in which to notify Able, the drawer.

(6) Notice sent but not received

Where notice of dishonour is duly addressed and posted the sender is deemed to have given due notice of dishonour notwithstanding any miscarriage by the post office.

S 50 specifies the circumstances in which delay in giving notice is excused and in which the giving of notice is excused altogether. These rules are set out under headings (1) and (2) below.

(1) Effect of delay

Delay in giving notice of dishonour is excused where the delay is caused by circumstances beyond the control of the party giving notice provided that the delay is not a result of his default, misconduct or negligence. When the cause of delay ceases to operate, the notice must be given with reasonable diligence.

(2) Notice of dishonour is dispensed with

(a) Where after the exercise of reasonable diligence notice cannot be given or does not reach the relevant drawer or indorser.

(b) Where notice is waived expressly or impliedly before notice is due or even after the failure to give notice.

(c) With respect to giving notice to the drawer where:

(i) He and the drawee are the same person (as with a banker's draft);

50

(ii) The drawee is a fictitious person or a person with no capacity to contract;

(iii) The drawer is the person to whom the bill is presented for payment;

(iv) The drawee or acceptor is under no obligation to the drawer to accept or pay the bill (as where the drawer of a cheque has insufficient funds in his bank account);

(v) The drawer has countermanded payment.

(d) With respect to giving notice to the indorser where:

(i) The drawee is a fictitious person or a person with no capacity to contract and the indorser was aware of either fact when he indorsed the bill;

(ii) The indorser is the person to whom the bill is presented for payment;

(iii) The bill was accepted or made for the accommodation of the indorser.

NOTING AND PROTESTING

The object of these formalities (which in practice are usually only invoked on the dishonour of foreign bills, thus bringing English Law into line with most other legal systems which insist on protest) is to obtain formal evidence of the fact that a bill has been dishonoured.

'Noting' is the procedure whereby a dishonoured bill is taken to a notary public who re-presents the bill. In the event of it being dishonoured again he 'notes', on the day of dishonour or the following business day, on the bill the date, a reference to his register, and his charges, and he attaches a ticket giving 'the answer he receives'. At a later date the notary may draw up a formal declaration giving details of the re-presentation and the result is the 'protest'. By S 51(7) the protest must contain a copy of the bill, be signed by the notary public, specify at whose request the bill is protested, and the place, date and reason for the protest.

Where an inland bill has been dishonoured, s 51(1) states that the holder *may* obtain a noting for non-acceptance or for non-payment, but the subsection states that neither noting nor protesting is necessary to preserve the liability of the drawer and indorsers of inland bills. But by s 51(2) where a bill which appears on its face to be a foreign bill (see page 11) has been dishonoured by non-acceptance it must be duly protested for non-acceptance, and where such a bill which has not been previously dishonoured by non-acceptance it must be duly protested for non-payment. If it is not protested in these circumstances, the drawer and indorsers are discharged unless protest is excused.

S 51(9) provides that protest is dispensed with by any circumstances which would dispense with notice of dishonour. Delay in noting or protesting is excused when the delay is caused by circumstances beyond the control of the holder, and is not imputable to his default, misconduct or negligence. When the cause of delay ceases to operate the bill must be noted or protested with reasonable diligence.

If the services of a notary cannot be obtained at the time and place of dishonour, any householder or substantial resident of the place may, in the presence of two witnesses, give a certificate, signed by them attesting the dishonour of the bill, and the certificate will operate in all respects as if it were a formal protest (s 94).

DAMAGES IN THE EVENT OF DISHONOUR

S 57 provides that where a bill is dishonoured the measure of liquidated damages is deemed to be:

(a) The amount of the bill;

(b) Interest from the maturity of the bill or presentment for payment if the bill is payable on demand;

(c) The expense of noting or, when protest is necessary and has been obtained, the expense of the protest.

The holder may recover the liquidated damages from any party liable on the bill and the drawer who has been compelled to pay the bill may recover from the acceptor. An indorser who has been compelled to pay the bill may recover from the acceptor or from the drawer or from a prior indorser.

The interest recoverable will be at the rate specified in the bill. If the bill fails to specify the rate, then the court may award interest, and in practice interest at 5 per cent until judgement is commonly awarded.

ACCEPTANCE AND PAYMENT FOR HONOUR

(This topic is dealt with in ss 65-68.) A bill of exchange protested for dishonour by non-acceptance or protested for better security which is not overdue may, with the consent of the holder, be accepted for the honour of any person liable on the bill who may, for instance, be insolvent either for the whole sum stated in the bill or a part of that sum. Such a person is referred to as 'the acceptor for honour *supra* protest'.

The acceptor for honour promises that he will, on due presentment, pay the bill if it is not paid by the drawee/acceptor provided the bill has been protested for non-payment and that he has been notified of these events.

Similarly, where a bill has been protested for non-payment any person may intervene and pay it for the honour of any person liable on the bill. The object is to prevent action being taken against the person for whose honour the bill has been accepted or paid.

In order that payment for honour constitutes a valid discharge of all parties subsequent to the party for whose honour it is paid, it must be attested by a notarial act of honour which must be attached to the protest made at the time of dishonour. The payer takes over the rights of that person against prior parties. The attestation provides evidence that the payment has been made and liability discharged, otherwise the payment could be claimed to be merely voluntary.

The notarial act of honour must contain a declaration made by the payer for honour that his intention is to pay the bill for honour and for whose honour he pays.

As has already been stated, where a bill has been paid for honour all parties subsequent to the party for whose honour it is paid are discharged. Thus:

> If payment is made to Quentin by Willing, a friend of Cain who is prepared to act for the honour of his friend, thus paying *supra* protest for the honour of Cain, then all parties who have indorsed the bill after Cain are discharged from liability. Thus Mark will be discharged from liability with respect to the bill. The parties subsequent to the party for whose honour it is paid are discharged but the payer for honour acquires the rights and duties of holder with respect to all the parties liable to the person for whose honour he accepts.
>
> Willing succeeds to the rights and duties of Cain. Willing can recover the money he has paid Quentin either from Brown (if Brown has previously accepted the bill) or from Able as drawer of the bill.

The payer for honour is entitled to receive the bill and protest from the holder when he has paid both the amount of the bill and the expenses of noting and protesting to the holder.

6 Discharge of a Bill

Discharge is the process whereby a bill of exchange ceases to have value or evidence rights for any party to the bill. Discharge of the *bill* must be distinguished from the situation where a *party* to the bill may be discharged, e.g. by a failure to give an indorser notice of dishonour, in which case that indorser may well be discharged. A bill may be discharged by a variety of events:

(1) By payment in due course (s 59(1));

(2) Where an accommodation bill is paid in due course by the party accommodated (s 59(3));

(3) When the acceptor of a bill is or becomes the holder of it at or after its maturity in his own right (s 61);

(4) When the holder of a bill at or after its maturity absolutely and unconditionally renounces his rights against the acceptor (s 62);

(5) Where a bill is intentionally cancelled (s 63);

(6) When a bill is altered (s 64).

We will now consider each of these methods of discharge in further detail.

PAYMENT IN DUE COURSE

S 3 requires that the drawee of a bill pays on demand or at a fixed or determinable future date a sum certain in money. When the drawee has fulfilled this requirement the bill is discharged. S 59(1) provides that 'A bill is discharged by payment in due course by or on behalf of the drawee or acceptor'.

Payment in due course is defined to mean payment made on or after maturity of the bill to the holder of the bill in good faith without notice that his title to the bill is defective. It should be remembered that a person (even if innocent) cannot qualify as a 'holder' if he is in possession of an order bill following a forged indorsement. Therefore if such a person is paid by the acceptor the bill is not discharged and the acceptor is still liable to pay the amount of the bill to the true owner (see page 33). Thus:

> If Brown pays Cain £800 on or after the date the bill matures the bill is discharged. Similarly, if Cain has negotiated the bill to Mark payment of the £800 to Mark on or after the date of maturity will discharge the bill provided that Brown has not received notice that Mark's title to the bill is defective.

Where a bill is paid by the drawer or an indorser (as opposed to the drawee/acceptor) it is not generally discharged, except:

(i) If the bill payable to or to the order of a third party is paid by the drawer the drawer may not reissue the bill but may enforce payment against the acceptor. Thus the bill is ineffective for future use and to all intents and purposes discharged, the only exception being the right of action between the drawer and acceptor.

(ii) Where a bill is paid by an indorser, or where a bill payable to drawer's order is paid by the drawer, the party paying it can pursue his rights against the acceptor or previous parties and he may strike out his own and later indorsements and negotiate the bill again.
  In such circumstances a number of parties to the bill may be discharged; the bill itself is not, however, discharged. Thus:

> If Mark negotiates the bill to Quentin, Quentin is then the holder of the bill, and as holder may obtain the £800 payment from Mark. Payment by Mark does not discharge the bill. Mark may (1) sue Brown for the £800, or (2) cross out his indorsement and negotiate the bill yet again.

PAYMENT OF ACCOMMODATION BILLS

The *bill* will only be discharged when it is paid in due course by the *party accommodated* (s 59(3)). Thus turning to the example on page 53, payment by Willing, the accommodation acceptor, will not discharge the bill because not all rights and liabilities under the bill would have been extinguished; Willing will now have a right to claim indemnity from Brown, the party whom he accommodated.

WHEN THE ACCEPTOR BECOMES THE HOLDER

When the acceptor of a bill is or becomes the holder of it, at or after its maturity, in his own right, the bill is discharged (s 61). Thus:

If Cain negotiated the bill to Mark and Mark in turn negotiates to Quentin who negotiates the bill to Brown and Brown has previously accepted the bill, the bill is discharged. Brown is both the person entitled to the £800 payment and the person liable to pay the £800. This is sometimes referred to as 'circuity of action'.

If the bill were negotiated to the acceptor *before* maturity, the bill is not discharged; the acceptor would be regarded as having discounted the bill and could re-issue it thereby rendering the drawer and indorser liable to subsequent holders.

EXPRESS WAIVER

Where the holder of the bill at or after its maturity absolutely and unconditionally renounces his rights against the acceptor, the bill is discharged. It is essential that the renunciation is absolute and unconditional. The renunciation must be in writing unless the bill itself is delivered to the acceptor (s 62(1)).

The holder may renounce the liability of any party to the bill before, at, or even after its maturity, but this will not affect the rights of the holder in due course who has no notice of the renunciation (s 62(2)). All the indorsers of a bill will be liable to the holder in due course unless the holder in due course has received notice that the liability of a particular party has been renounced.

CANCELLATION

When a *bill* is intentionally cancelled by a holder or his agent and the cancellation is apparent on the face of the bill, the bill is discharged (s 63(1)).

A cancellation made unintentionally or under a mistake or without the authority of the holder is inoperative. Where a bill appears to have been cancelled it is for the party who alleges that the cancellation has been made unintentionally, under a mistake or without authority, to prove it (s 63(3)).

Similarly, that holder of a bill can intentionally cancel the liability of *a party to the bill*. When this occurs, any indorser who would have had a right of recourse against the party whose signature is cancelled is also discharged (s 63(2)). The *bill* itself is not, however, discharged in these circumstances. Thus:

If Quentin intentionally cancels the liability of Cain, Mark is also discharged from liability with respect to the bill because he would have had a right of recourse against Cain.

ALTERATION OF A BILL

Where a bill or acceptance is materially altered without the assent of all the parties liable on the bill the bill is avoided and thus discharged except as against a party who has made, authorised or assented to the alteration and subsequent indorsers (s 64(1)).

The alteration of the date, the sum payable, the time of payment, the place of payment and, if the bill has been accepted generally, the addition of a place of payment without the acceptor's consent will all constitute material alterations which therefore may avoid the bill. This applies also, of course, to cheques; furthermore, the alteration of the word 'order' to 'bearer' (but not vice versa) and any deletion in the crossing on a cheque would be considered a material alteration. The drawer of a cheque, however, owes a contractual duty of care to the bank to take all reasonable care when drawing up the cheque (see *London Joint Stock Bank* v. *Macmillan & Arthur*, page 74). A bill is not avoided by immaterial alterations.

However, if the alteration is not apparent then should the bill be in the hands of a holder in due course he may treat the bill as if it had not been materially altered and may enforce payment according to the original order (s 64(1)). Thus:

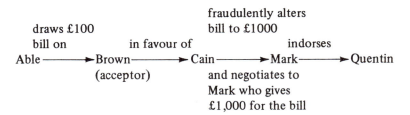

It follows that if the alteration is apparent Quentin will have no rights against Able and Brown, but he can sue Cain, who made the alteration and Mark, a subsequent indorser, for the £1,000 that he gave for the bill.

But if the alteration is not apparent Quentin is given further rights if he qualifies as a holder in due course of the bill. Not only will he be able to enforce the bill for £1,000 against Cain and Mark, but Quentin will also be able to make Able and Brown liable for £100 (the original tenor). This is valuable if, for instance, Cain and Mark were insolvent. In practice, therefore, Quentin would claim his £1,000 from Mark; Mark would be entitled to claim £1,000 from Cain if he can be found; failing that, the unfortunate Mark would only be able to claim £100 from Able or Brown, losing £900 as a consquence of the alteration.

57

7 The Nature of a Cheque

S 73 provides that a cheque is a bill of exchange drawn on a banker payable on demand. SS 73 to 81 (Part III of the Bills of Exchange Act, 1882) lay down particular provisions which apply to cheques; otherwise a cheque is to be regarded as a bill of exchange payable on demand and the principles of law relating to demand bills will apply to a cheque.

The drawee of a cheque must always be a banker. Somewhat unhelpfully, s 2 defines a banker as one who carries on the business of banking, but authorities such as 'Paget' and 'Byles' agree that the acceptance of deposits on current accounts, the payment of cheques drawn on such accounts and the collection of cheques for customers as the major part of the business would constitute a carrying on of the business of banking.

The basic relationship between a bank and its customer is one of debtor and creditor. While a customer's account is in credit the bank is the debtor and the customer the creditor. In an overdrawn account situation the bank is the creditor and the customer the debtor. In any event, there is a contract between a customer and his bank. That bank must be named as the drawee in any order written in the form of a cheque by the customer, the drawer.

The customer of a bank is issued with a book of cheques on which to write his orders to the bank. The customer is the drawer of the cheques. The orders written by the customer may take the form of:

(a) An instruction to the bank to pay a specified amount of money from the customer's account to the customer. This instruction is frequently found in the form of 'Pay cash' or 'Pay cash or order'.

NORTH & SOUTH INSURANCE CORPORATION v. NATIONAL PROVINCIAL BANK LTD (1936) 1 KB 328

The instruction 'Pay cash' was *held* to be a direct order by a customer to his bank in reliance upon their contract. A bill of exchange is defined to require that a certain sum of money is ordered to be paid to a specified person or to bearer. The order 'Pay cash' does not satisfy s 3; such an order is not a bill of exchange and therefore not a cheque.

(b) An instruction to the bank to pay a certain amount of money to a third party.

Continuing our example, the drawee is a bank by the name of Brown Bank Ltd, the drawer is Able and the payee Cain. If Able completes a cheque from the book of cheques supplied by Brown Bank Ltd which state that Brown Bank Ltd is the drawee and Able completes the cheque making the sum therein stated £800 payable to Cain, that instrument is a bill of exchange. It is a bill drawn on a banker and (subject to being payable on demand) a cheque.

Cheques are subject to the rules of negotiation in exactly the same way as all other bills of exchange.

The second requirement of s 73 is that the bill of exchange must be payable on demand in order to qualify as a cheque. Bills of exchange generally may be payable:

(1) On demand, or

(2) At a fixed future time, or

(3) At a determinable future time.

The strict rules relating to the date of payment of bills of exchange do not apply to cheques. A cheque will be dated by the drawer. From the date inserted by the drawer the payee has six years in which to enforce the order. This is the maximum period allowed for bringing an action in contract as stipulated by the Statute of Limitation, 1939.

Taking the s 3 definition of a bill of exchange a cheque is:

— An unconditional order in writing
— addressed by one person, the drawer, to a bank
— signed by the drawer
— requiring the bank to pay on demand
— a sum certain in money
— to or to the order of a specified person or to bearer.

The analysis of s 3 given in Chapter 3 for the most part applies equally to cheques. A cheque is a particular type of a bill of exchange.

Nevertheless two further points should be made in consequence of this definition:

(i) 'Travellers' cheques are probably not cheques because they are not 'unconditional'; they are usually drawn on condition that they are counter-signed by the holder in the presence of the paying bank or other agent.

(ii) Strictly speaking, a post-dated cheque is not a cheque since it is not payable on demand; indeed a banker must be very careful to recognise such documents because the drawer of a post-dated cheque may 'stop' or 'countermand' payment at any time before the date stated, and a banker who pays before the specified date stands to lose the money.

DAMAGES IN THE EVENT OF INSOLVENCY OF DRAWER'S BANK

S 74 provides that where a cheque is not presented for payment within a reasonable time of its issue and the drawer, or the person on whose account it is drawn, had the right at the time of such presentment as between him and the banker to have the cheque paid and suffers actual damage through the delay, he is discharged to the extent of such damage, that is, to the extent to which the drawer is a creditor of the bank to a larger amount than he would have been if the cheque had been paid. In such a case the holder may obtain judgement for that amount against the banker.

The damage envisaged by this section will only occur if the drawee bank becomes insolvent during the period of time when a cheque has been issued but has not been encashed. Such an event is extremely unlikely to occur today. Thus:

> Able, with £1,000 in his account with Brown Bank, draws a cheque in favour of Cain for £400. Cain takes more than a reasonable time before paying the cheque into his account, and, in the meantime, Brown Bank goes into liquidation and is only able to pay 25 pence in the pound. Able will be regarded as a creditor of the bank for £600 and Cain for £400. The result is that Able will receive £150 in the liquidation and Cain, £100. Able's liability to Cain will be discharged — hence the importance of presenting cheques promptly.

Apart from the (unlikely) insolvency of the bank, a cheque, by banking practice, is usually regarded as 'stale' if it has not been presented for payment within six months of the date when it was drawn, and the bank may well insist on it being re-drawn.

In determining what is a reasonable time for the purpose of s 74 and therefore whether the issue of a particular cheque falls within the protection of the section regard must be paid to the nature of the instrument, the practice of the relevant trade and of the bank, and of the facts of the particular case (s 74(2)).

DETERMINATION OF BANKER'S AUTHORITY

The duty and authority of a bank to pay a cheque drawn on him by his customer are determined by:

60

(a) Countermand of payment. By countermanding payment a customer is cancelling a particular order he has written which, by definition, must be addressed to his bank (s 73) and is payable to a third party; to be effective the countermand must actually be bought to the notice of the banker. Furthermore, the bank is not required to act upon an unauthenticated telegram or telephone call, though the banker may treat such a message as justifying the postponement of the honouring of a cheque pending an inquiry into the genuineness of the message.

CURTICE v. LONDON CITY AND MIDLAND BANK (1908) 1 KB 293

Curtice sent a telegram to his bank at 5.30 p.m. countermanding payment of a cheque he had drawn that same day. At 6.15 p.m. the messenger boy put the telegram in the bank letter box (the bank having closed). Due to an oversight by the bank's employees, two days elapsed before the telegram was brought to the notice of the manager; meanwhile the cheque had been paid. It was *held* by the Court of Appeal that as the banker had no actual notice of the countermand the bank was not liable (the customer did not sue the bank in negligence — there may have been liability under that heading!).

The countermand must be sent to the branch of the bank at which the customer's account is actually kept. Thus in *London Provincial and South Western Bank Ltd* v. *Buszard* (1918) 35 TLR 142 it was *held* that notice of the stop given to one branch did not prevent another branch at which the account was kept, and which did not know of the countermand, from debiting that account.

BURNETT v. WESTMINSTER BANK LTD (1966) 1 QB 742

It was *held* that if a customer alters the branch of the bank on which he intends to draw on the cheque form issued by another branch, then a stop notified to the branch named in the alteration will be effective. (However, the bank may require the customer, as part of his contract, that he will not alter cheque forms: this will be binding.)

Where the bank mistakenly overlooks the drawer's countermand instructions the bank acts without mandate, and the money, being paid under a mistake of fact, is *prima facie* recoverable from the payee (or indorsee) (*Barclays Bank Ltd* v. *W.J. Sims and Son* and *Cooke (Southern) Ltd and Sowman* (1979) 129 *New Law Journal* 835).

(b) On notice of the customer's mental incapacity;

(c) On notice of an act of bankruptcy on which a bankruptcy petition could be presented against him;

(d) Making of a receiving order in bankruptcy;

(e) On notice of commencement of winding-up proceedings if the customer is a registered company;

(f) On service of a garnishee order *nisi* on the account; this order directs a person (here the bank) who owes money to a judgement debtor (the customer) to freeze the judgement debtor's account in favour of the judgement creditor; cheques drawn by the customer will not be paid by the bank;

(g) Knowledge of any defect in the title of the presenter, since the bank must pay in good faith; and for similar reasons —

(h) Knowledge that the customer is drawing the cheque for an unlawful purpose, or that, if a trustee, in breach of a trust.

(i) Notice of the customer's death. Until the bank receives a reliable notice of the death of one of its customers it is entitled to debit that customer's account with the sum stated in the order. Notice of death operates as a countermand of payment thenceforth.

THE PAYING AND COLLECTING BANKS

It is important to identify that the use of cheques generally involves two customers and two banks. Thus:

> We have a customer, Able, and his bank is Brown Bank Ltd. If Able draws a crossed cheque payable to Cain, Cain will have to pay the cheque into his own bank account at the Smith Bank Ltd in order to obtain payment under that order. Cain's bank is the collecting bank in these circumstances. Smith Bank Ltd will collect the amount stated in the order from Able's bank, Brown Bank Ltd. Brown Bank Ltd is the paying bank.

All banks act on behalf of their customers, as the agent of their customer, to collect the proceeds on cheques paid into the account and as paying bank with respect to orders drawn by the customer. Banks do receive some statutory protection when acting as a collecting agent or paying agent (see Chapter 10).

THE FORM OF A CHEQUE

Typically a cheque is printed and completed in the following form:

Brown Bank Ltd	(Date)
22 Money Street, London	
Pay (the name of the payee)	or order
(the amount written in words)	£0.00
	(Drawer's signature)

On the cheque there will also be printed:

(1) The number of the cheque;

(2) The code number of the drawee bank;

(3) The drawer's account number.

All these numbers are written in magnetic ink which can be interpreted by computers. Computers have become a vital part of the process of banking.

DISTINCTIONS BETWEEN CHEQUES AND OTHER BILLS

(1) A cheque must always be drawn on a banker and always be payable on demand. A bill may be drawn on anyone and may be made payable on demand or at a fixed or determinable future time.

(2) A cheque may be crossed in several ways (see Chapter 8). Bills cannot be crossed.

(3) A cheque is never accepted. The contract between a customer and his bank provides that the bank will pay according to the instructions given in the form of a cheque. The liability of the banker is to his customer, the drawer. The banker is never liable to the holder of a cheque. A bill of exchange may be accepted. After acceptance the acceptor is primarily liable to the holder of the bill.

(4) When a cheque is returned to the holder for any reason no notice of dishonour is necessary in order to claim against the drawer. Want of assets

on the part of the drawer is sufficient reason for return, and the drawee's act of returning the cheque is deemed to be sufficient notice of dishonour with respect to the holder. When a bill is dishonoured for non-acceptance or non-payment, notice must be given in accordance with the Act, otherwise the liability of the parties to the bill is discharged.

(5) A banker who pays a cheque drawn to order which bears a forged or unauthorised indorsement is not liable to the true owner or to his customer if he pays the amount stated in the cheque in good faith and in the ordinary course of business (see Chapter 10). The drawee of a bill obtains no protection if he pays a bill bearing a forged indorsement. He is still liable to the true owner of the bill (see Chapter 4).

(6) Presentment of a cheque for payment within a reasonable time of its issue will not discharge the drawer unless he suffers actual loss (see page 60); on the other hand, a bill payable on demand must be presented for payment to the drawee within a reasonable time after its issue, otherwise the drawer is discharged.

8 Crossings

Crossings are peculiar to cheques. The crossing must be placed on the face of the cheque, and s 76 explains the various types of crossing which are of legal significance:

(1) Simply two parallel transverse lines;

(2) Two parallel transverse lines and between the lines the words 'and Company' or 'and Co.';

(3) Two parallel transverse lines and between the lines the words 'and Company' (or the abbreviation) and the words 'not negotiable';

(4) Two parallel transverse lines and between the lines the words 'and Company' (or the abbreviation) and the name of a banker;

(5) Two parallel transverse lines and between the lines the words 'and Company' (or the abbreviation), the words 'not negotiable' and the name of a banker.

The type of crossing described in (1), (2) and (3) above are described as general, whereas examples (4) and (5) constitute special crossings.

When a customer of a bank requests crossed cheque forms from his bank they are invariably printed with two parallel transverse lines and, in the case of some, but not all banks, with the words '& Co.' printed between the lines.

A GENERAL CROSSING

Where the banker on whom a cheque is drawn pays a cheque crossed generally other than to a banker he is liable to the true owner of the cheque for any loss he may sustain owing to the cheque being paid other than to a banker (s 79(2)).

The effect of placing two parallel transverse lines across the face of a cheque (with or without the words '& Co.' written between those lines) is to ensure that the amount stated payable in the cheque is paid into a bank account and is not paid by a banker as cash over the counter on presentation of the cheque. If a banker does pay cash over the counter on a crossed cheque and he has not paid the true owner of the cheque he will remain liable to the true owner.

If Able draws a generally crossed cheque for £800 made payable to Cain using one of the cheque forms provided by the Brown Bank Ltd it will take the following form:

Brown Bank Ltd 22 Money Street, London	*& Co.*	13 November 1979
Pay Cain		or order
the sum of eight hundred pounds		£800
		Able (signature)

When Cain presents the generally crossed cheque drawn by Able to his bank it will refuse to give him cash for that cheque but will act as his agent and collect the £800 from the Brown Bank Ltd and then credit Cain's account with the £800 as ordered by Able. The crossing therefore gives some protection against theft in that the holder (Cain) has additional time to contact Able and have the cheque stopped if Cain discovers that the cheque has been stolen from him.

A SPECIAL CROSSING

S 79(2) also provides that where a banker on whom a cheque is drawn pays a cheque crossed specially otherwise than to the banker to whom it is crossed (or that bank's agent for collection) he is liable to the true owner of the cheque for any loss sustained by the true owner as a result of the cheque being paid other than to the banker named in the crossing.

A special crossing is immediately recognisable because the name of the collecting bank will be written between the two parallel transverse lines on the face of the cheque. Where a cheque is crossed specially to more than one banker the banker on whom it is drawn should refuse payment unless the second-named bank is merely acting as agent for the first-named bank for the purpose of collecting the proceeds (s 79(1)). This provision was more relevant in the past, where many banks were not collecting banks and such banks would use a major London bank as agent for the collection of cheques through the bankers' clearing system. A bank that is not a collecting bank will therefore need to rely upon an authorised collecting bank in order to collect the proceeds as ordered in the cheque on behalf of their customers. Thus:

If Able draws a cheque payable to Cain and specially crosses the cheque naming the Smith Bank Ltd as the collecting bank it will take the following form:

Brown Bank Ltd		25 May 1979
22 Money Street, London		
Pay Cain		or order
the sum of eight hundred pounds	*Smith Bank Ltd & Co.*	£800
		Able
		(signature)

The Brown Bank Ltd will remain liable to the true owner of the cheque, Cain, if it makes payment other than to the Smith Bank Ltd. If, for example, the above cheque is stolen by X and presented by X for payment to the Z Bank Ltd for collection and the Brown Bank Ltd pays the £800 to the Z Bank Ltd the Brown Bank Ltd will still be liable to Cain. The Brown Bank Ltd must pay the Smith Bank Ltd or the bank acting as agent for collection for the Smith Bank Ltd in order to discharge its liability to Cain.

CROSSING 'ACCOUNT PAYEE'

If the words 'account payee' or 'account payee only' are written between the two parallel transverse lines on the face of the cheque, although not constituting a crossing recognised by the Act, it will be effective to afford the true owner of the cheque greater protection. The collecting bank is thereby under a duty to make inquiry to see that it collects for the payee named in the cheque or that its customer has the payee's authority to collect. Failure to make such inquiry will render the bank liable to the true owner. This is somewhat academic, because in practice a banker is unlikely to collect such cheques for an account other than that of the named payee.

Such a crossing does not affect the negotiability of the cheque.

CROSSING 'NOT NEGOTIABLE'

S 81 provides that where a person takes a crossed cheque which bears within the crossing the words 'not negotiable' he shall not have and shall not be capable of giving a better title to the cheque than that possessed by the person from whom he took it.

It will be recalled that a restrictive indorsement on a bill gives the indorsee the right to receive payment on the bill but gives him no power to transfer his rights as indorsee unless the instrument expressly authorises him to do so. Thus the words 'not negotiable' written on a bill will prevent any further transfer of that bill. It seems, however, that a cheque can continue to be negotiated notwithstanding the words 'not negotiable' written across the face of the cheque, so long as the words do not appear as part of a crossing. Once the words 'not negotiable' are added to the crossing any subsequent holder of the cheque can receive no better title to it than the transferor, but the cheque remains transferable. Thus:

> If Able adds the words 'not negotiable' to his general crossing then the cheque can only be negotiated by Cain or subsequent indorsers subject to the principle that no-one can pass a better title than he himself possesses; in other words, the transfer will be 'subject to equities'. Able may also add the words 'not negotiable' to a special crossing with a like effect.

The object in crossing a cheque is to ensure that the person intended to receive payment of the order as drawn does, in fact, receive payment. At the same time, a cheque is a bill of exchange and therefore essentially a negotiable instrument. Hence the option of adding the words 'not negotiable'.

CROSSINGS AFTER ISSUE

A cheque may be crossed generally or specially at any of various stages in the drawing and negotiating of a cheque. Thus a cheque may be crossed:

(1) When it is being drawn up.

(2) When negotiated uncrossed. The rightful holder of an uncrossed cheque may add a general or special crossing to the cheque.

(3) When negotiated with a general crossing. The rightful holder of a generally crossed cheque may add the name of a bank between the two transverse parallel lines thus stipulating the collecting bank. The crossing thereby becomes a special crossing.

In any event, where a cheque is crossed generally or specially, the holder may add the words 'not negotiable'. Thus:

> If Able, when drawing up the cheque made payable to Cain, adds two transverse parallel lines and whether or not between those lines he writes '& Co', the cheque will be generally crossed. The effect of this crossing is to ensure that no person can receive cash directly from a bank on presenting the cheque. Cain, before he negotiates this cheque to Mark, may either:
>
> (a) Specify the bank who will collect the proceeds for Mark. Such a crossing will not, however, prevent Mark from negotiating the cheque further; or
>
> (b) Add the words 'not negotiable' to the crossing. Such an instruction will not prevent the cheque being negotiated further than Mark but all subsequent holders of that cheque can acquire no better title to it than that of the transferor.
>
> Cain may simply indorse the cheque to Mark and add nothing to the existing crossings. In that event (a) and (b) above will be the options available to Mark.

Where an uncrossed cheque or a cheque crossed generally is given to a banker for collection that banker may cross the cheque specially to himself (s 77(6)). A cheque crossed specially to a banker can be crossed by that banker specially to another banker for collection (s 77(5)). These and all the crossings mentioned earlier in this chapter form a material part of the cheque.

It is unlawful for any unauthorised person to obliterate, add to or alter the crossing (s 78). Material alteration of the cheque without the assent of all parties liable avoids the cheque except as against a party who has made, authorised or assented to the alteration and except as against subsequent indorsers (see page 57). The cancellation of crossings, as where a customer wishes to draw cash from his bank account and uses his printed crossed cheque form, makes the cheque payable to 'cash' and writes the words such as 'please pay cash' over the crossing and signing it, is not authorised by statute. However, in practice banks will cash such cheques for the drawer or his known agent, e.g. his wife.

However, where a cheque is presented for payment which does not at the time of presentment appear to be crossed, or to have had a crossing which has been obliterated, or to have been added to or altered otherwise than as authorised by the Act, the banker paying the cheque in good faith and without negligence shall not be responsible or incur any liability and the payment made cannot be questioned (s 79(2), proviso).

SCOPE OF THE RULES AS TO CROSSINGS

The above rules apply to the following documents as well as to cheques, strictly defined:

(1) Conditional orders (e.g. 'pay Cain provided he signs a receipt'), and 'pay cash' documents;

(2) Bankers' drafts;

(3) Dividend warrants;

(4) Documents issued by a public officer and which are intended to enable a person to obtain payment from the Paymaster General or the Queen's and Lord Treasurer's Remembrancer of the sum mentioned in the document but which is not a bill of exchange.

9 Relationship between Banker and Customer

There are two basic relationships between a banker and his customer — that of debtor and creditor and that of principal and agent. If a person's money is accepted by a bank he, the customer, is the creditor and the bank undertakes to honour cheques up to the amount standing to a customer's credit in return for being able in the meantime to use the customer's money. If the banker agrees to extend overdraft facilities to the customer either formally or by honouring cheques when the customer's account contains no money then the debtor/creditor relationship is reversed and it is the customer who is the debtor.

As a contract exists between a banker and his customer the banker will be liable for breach of contract, if, without lawful justification, he refuses or fails to pay a cheque presented to him.

The debt owed by a banker to a customer is, like all other debts, subject to the Statute of Limitation and therefore barred after six years. This time period does not, however, run from the opening of the current account but from the rejection of the particular demand for repayment.

JOACHIMSON v. SWISS BANK CORPORATION [1921] 3 KB 110

A partnership consisting of two Germans and one Englishman was carrying on business in England. One of the German partners died, and the partnership was thus dissolved; at that time the partnership bank account stood in credit to £2,321. Three days later, on the outbreak of the First World War (4 August 1914) the remaining German partner became an enemy alien. Five years later the Englishman in the name of the partnership sought to recover the £2,321 from the bank, it being alleged that the cause of action had arisen on or before 1 August 1914. No demand for repayment had been made on or before that date and the bank pleaded that as there had accrued no cause of action to the firm on 1 August 1914, the action was not maintainable. The Court of Appeal *held* that where money was standing to a customer's credit on current account at a bank a previous demand was necessary before an action could be maintained against the bank for the money; judgement was therefore given for the bank.

With a *deposit account* it is usually a condition that the customer must give several days' notice of his desire to withdraw; in these circumstances time does not begin to run against him until the period of notice has expired.

OPENING THE ACCOUNT

The contract between a banker and a customer will only be entered into after careful consideration by the banker as to the suitability of the proposed customer. Bankers pursue references to assist them with their decision. A bank may well lose its statutory protection afforded by both the Bills of Exchange Act, 1882 and the Cheques Act, 1957 if it is negligent (see Chapter 10). A bank's failure to take up references or failure to check references when opening an account have been held to be negligent acts.

LADBROKE & CO. v. TODD (1914) 19 Com Cas 256

The plaintiff posted a cheque crossed 'Account payee only' in payment of a betting win to Jobson. The cheque was stolen in the course of post and the thief posing as Jobson opened an account at the defendant bank, paid in the cheque and withdrew the same amount. It was *held* that the bank was negligent in failing to observe the common practice of obtaining references, and so the bank had to repay the proceeds of the cheque to the rightful owner.

HAMPSTEAD GUARDIANS v. BARCLAYS BANK LTD (1923) 39 TLR 229

Two cheques were drawn by the plaintiffs in favour of D. Stewart & Co. These cheques were stolen and a man posing as Donald Stewart opened an account with Barclays Bank and gave a Mr Woolf as a reference. The bank was given a satisfactory reference from Mr Woolf, but the reference was, in fact, forged. The bank did not check the name and address of the customer nor of the referee. The court *held* that the bank's conduct was negligent; the bank was therefore required to repay the proceeds of the cheques.

MARFANI & CO. v. MIDLAND BANK LTD [1968] 2 All ER 573

Marfani's office manager, Kureshy, prepared a cheque for £3,000 payable to Eliaszade. Kureshy obtained the signature of his employer on the cheque and then, posing as Eliaszade, opened an account at the Midland Bank giving as reference a man who knew him as Eliaszade. Kureshy withdrew the money from the account and left the country. The Court of Appeal *held* that on those facts the following acts did not amount to negligence:

(1) The bank not enquiring further about the referee (he himself had been a customer of the bank for six years) nor the fact of there only being one referee.

(2) The bank not asking for evidence of identity nor enquiring as to the new customer's employment in view of the reference.

(3) The clearance of the cheque before the reference was received.

The basic contractual relationship between banker and customer enables the customer to withdraw money from or pay into his account by giving the requisite order to his bank. It will be recalled (see page 58) that a cheque made payable to 'Cash' is not a valid bill of exchange. Thus:

> If Able should drawn an instrument on the Brown Bank Ltd payable to 'Cash' then that instrument is a valid binding order as between Able and his bank, the Brown Bank Ltd, but is not a negotiable instrument. Such an order is neither a cheque nor a bill of exchange.

AGENCY

The relationship of banker and customer is also one of agent and principal. The bank acts as the agent of its customer in two situations:

(1) As agent to pay money out of his principal's account whenever the principal should choose to write an order for the benefit of a third party. Thus:

> Able is the principal and Brown Bank Ltd his agent. If Able draws a cheque made payable to Cain the Brown Bank Ltd will act as the agent of Able by paying the amount stated in the cheque to Cain.

(2) As agent to collect money on behalf of his customer whenever the customer pays into his account cheques drawn by a third party. Thus:

> If Cain pays that cheque into his account at the Smith Bank Ltd, then the Smith Bank Ltd will act as Cain's agent by collecting the amount stated in the cheque from Brown Bank Ltd.

In *Joachimson* v. *Swiss Bank Corporation*, Lord Justice Atkin described the customer/banker relationship: 'The bank undertakes to receive money and to collect bills for its customer's account. The proceeds so received are not to be held in trust for the customer, but the bank borrows the proceeds and undertakes to repay them. The promise to repay is to repay at the branch of

73

the bank where the account is kept, and during banking hours. It includes a promise to repay any part of the amount due against the written order of the customer addressed to the bank at the branch.'

Thus two relationships exist between a banker and his customer:

(1) A debtor/creditor contractual relationship; and

(2) A principal and agent contractual relationship.

Both the customer and the banker are bound by certain duties in carrying out and fulfilling those contracts. Thus we can study the duties of care owed by a customer to his banker and the duties owed by a banker to his customer.

THE CUSTOMER'S DUTIES OF CARE

(1) A customer owes a duty of care to his banker not to draw up his cheques carelessly.

YOUNG v. GROTE (1827) 4 Bing 253

A customer carelessly drew up a cheque for £50 so as to enable the holder to change the words and figures up to £150. £150 was paid by the customer's bank. The court *held* that although a bank cannot normally debit a customer's account with respect to orders which have been materially altered (unless all the parties to the order have authorised and agreed to the alteration (s 64(2)) the bank can debit a customer's account where the cheque is carelessly drawn.

LONDON JOINT STOCK BANK v. MACMILLAN & ARTHUR [1918] AC 777

A clerk whose job it was to prepare cheques for his employer to sign made out a cheque for £2 payable to M (a specified person) or to bearer. The clerk did not fill in the amount in words and left a space before the figure '2'. After the cheque was signed the clerk raised the amount to £120, filled in the words, encashed the cheque at the bank and absconded with the proceeds. The House of Lords *held* that the bank was entitled to debit the employer's account with the full amount of £120, the customer being in breach of duty in failing to exercise reasonable care in drawing up the cheques to ensure that the *banker is not misled*.

However, the Court of Appeal *held* in *Slingsby* v. *District Bank Ltd* (1932)

74

1 KB 544, that the drawer was under no duty to fill in the space on the cheque between the payee's name and the printed words 'or order' by drawing a line; therefore the bank has no right to debit the drawer's account when the payee's name has been fraudulently altered by the addition of words between that name as originally written and the words 'or order'.

Perhaps a court would decide differently today when it is more usual for a drawer of a cheque to fill in the gap after the payee's name.

(2) A customer owes a duty to his banker to inform the bank should he discover that a person is forging his signature, otherwise he may be estopped from denying the validity of the signature.

GREENWOOD v. MARTINS BANK LTD [1933] AC 51

A wife forged her husband's signature. The husband knew of his wife's forgeries. The court *held* that the husband by his silence had deprived the bank of its right of action against the forger and was therefore unable to claim from the bank the £410 his wife had obtained by forging his signature (see page 33).

A customer is required to do what he reasonably can to protect the banker. The banker, however, remains exposed to a variety of possible situations resulting in a loss, hence the statutory protection afforded to bankers by s 60 and s 80, Bills of Exchange Act, 1882 and by the Cheques Act, 1957 (see Chapter 10). A customer will not be liable to the bank if he fails to detect an error in his bank statement; he is under no duty to the bank to check that statement; indeed if the customer believes the credit balance shown in his statement to be correct, and he is not negligent, he can draw cheques to the full amount shown, the bank being estopped as the result of having produced the statement (*Holland* v. *Manchester & Liverpool Banking Co.* (1909) 25 TLR 386).

In *United Overseas Bank* v. *Jiwani* [1977] 1 All ER 733 it was *held* that to be entitled to rely on estoppel here the customer must also satisfy the court that it was his belief in his credit balance being as high as shown in the statement that caused him to have drawn cheques for the amount in question.

THE BANKER'S DUTIES TO THE CUSTOMER

(1) A banker has a duty to pay on a cheque drawn by his customer provided that the banker has funds in his hands belonging to the drawer in the form of a credit balance or agreed overdraft limit. It has just been seen that the bank may also be bound to honour cheques up to any further amount that he has misled the customer into believing he has in the account by an error in his statement. If the banker fails in this duty he will be liable in an action brought

by his customer for wrongful dishonour. If the customer is not a trader he will normally only be able to recover nominal damages in this event.

GIBBONS v. WESTMINSTER BANK LTD [1939] 2 KB 882

G, who was not a trader, paid into her bank account a sum of money which at the error of the bank was credited to another customer's account. G then issued a cheque in payment of her rent. This cheque was dishonoured by the bank under the impression that there were insufficient funds to meet it. The court *held* that because G was not a trader and had not proved any special damage she was entitled to nominal damages only.

However, in the case of a tradesman, and probably professional persons, the wrongful dishonour of a cheque may well lead to the award of substantial damages. It may also be possible to bring an action for libel against the bank as well as for breach of contract.

DAVIDSON v. BARCLAY'S BANK LTD [1940] 1 All ER 316

The plaintiff, a bookmaker, drew a cheque for £2.78*p*. which the bank erroneously returned to the payee marked 'not sufficient' across its face. It was *held* that the plaintiff was entitled to substantial damages of £250 for libel.

The banker is not bound to pay a cheque unless the full amount of the cheque can be covered by the customer's credit balance or agreed overdraft; thus a cheque drawn for £1,000 by a customer with a credit balance of £900 and no overdraft facility should either be refused payment or paid in full — the bank should not pay the cheque as to £900. The circumstances when the banker's duty to honour cheques terminates have already been discussed (see pages 60-62).

(2) A banker has a duty to make payments out of his customer's account only on the customer's signature and in accordance with the customer's order. (This duty is, however, mitigated by the statutory protection afforded to bankers.)

It follows from this duty that there is no mandate from the customer when the customer's signature *as drawer* is forged and the banker has no right to debit the customer's account. If the banker does make a payment on a forged cheque then usually the bank can recover the money from the recipient.

The payment by the banker of a forged cheque does not constitute a representation by the banker that a forged signature is genuine so as to pre-

76

clude or estop him from recovering the money paid to the recipients.

NATIONAL WESTMINSTER BANK LTD v. BARCLAYS BANK INTERNATIONAL LTD [1975] QB 654

Mr I purchased a cheque for £8,000, at a premium, drawn on the account of a customer of the National Westminster Bank. Mr I paid the cheque into his own account at Barclays. Barclays collected the proceeds and credited Mr I's account. Subsequently it was discovered that the cheque had been stolen from the owner's cheque book and skillfully forged. The National Westminster Bank brought an action to recover the money from Barclays. Mr I argued that because the cheque had been honoured the National Westminster Bank had represented that the cheque was valid and that therefore they could not recover the money from Barclays Bank International. The court *held* that payment does not constitute an implied representation that the signature is genuine. The National Westminster Bank were therefore held to be entitled to recover the money which had been paid under a mistake of fact.

Breach by the customer of his duty of care (see page 74) may save the bank which pays a cheque not signed by a customer. The bank may also be rescued by the equitable doctrine of subrogation which operates to prevent the customer from profiting from the wrongful payment. Thus:

LIGGETT (LIVERPOOL) LTD v. BARCLAYS BANK LTD [1928] 1 KB 48

The company had instructed its bankers that cheques drawn on the company's account were to be signed by two directors. The bank carelessly paid cheques signed by one director only. It was *held* that the bank was not entitled to debit the company's account, but on restoring the money to the customer, the bank was entitled to stand in the shoes of those creditors of the company who had been paid in breach of the banker's mandate.

It is very common for two people to open a joint account; the question that arises in the present context is what is the effect if the signature of one of the joint account holders is forged by the other? In *Brewer* v. *Westminster Bank Ltd* [1952] 2 All ER 650, it was held that since the bank's duties were owed jointly to the holders of a joint account, the forgery by one account-holder of the other's signature to cheques precluded a successful action against the bank; no action could be maintained unless each of the account-holders was in a position to sue, which clearly was not the case in *Brewer*, since the forger had no right to sue.

The law here is, however, very uncertain. Thus in *Jackson* v. *White and Midland Bank Ltd* [1967] 2 Lloyd's Rep. 68 (another decision at first instance) it was *held* that the bank agreed with each account-holder that it would not honour cheques unless signed by him; the consequences being that the bank will be liable to that account-holder whose signature is forged by the other, the bank duly honouring the cheque. Academic writers favour this opinion, and it seems unlikely that *Brewer* will be followed in the future.

(3) The banker has a duty to keep secret the affairs of his customer.

TOURNIER v. NATIONAL PROVINCIAL & UNION BANK OF ENGLAND [1924] 1 KB 461

Tournier had defaulted upon a written agreement to repay his overdraft to his bank by weekly payments. The bank manager telephoned Tournier's employer to find out Tournier's address and in the course of conversation disclosed that Tournier's account was overdrawn and that he was in breach of the agreement to repay his overdraft. Tournier consequently lost his employment and sued the bank for slander and for breach of implied contract not to disclose the state of his account or his transactions. The court *held* that the bank had a legal duty not to disclose to third persons the state of their customer's accounts.

Four qualifications to this basic principle of secrecy were recognised in the above case:

(a) Where disclosure is, by law, compulsory. For example, a bank is required to make a return to the Inland Revenue disclosing interest paid to customers and the Bankers' Books Evidence Act, 1879 allows the court to make an order authorising a party to an action to inspect entries in a banker's books.

(b) Where there is a public duty to disclose, e.g. where a customer is trading with an enemy in wartime.

(c) Where the interests of the bank require disclosure, as when, for example, the bank is calling upon a guarantor. The bank should not, however, disclose to the guarantor the amount by which the debt owed to the customer exceeds the guarantee.

(d) Where the disclosure is made with the express or implied consent of the customer, e.g. where the customer gives his banker as a reference.

(4) The banker has a duty to keep its customers correctly informed as to their financial position.

LLOYDS BANK LTD v. BROOKS (1950) JIB Vol. 72, 114

A customer was wrongly credited with a dividend by the bank's investment department. The bank had paid £1,108 over a number of years before the mistake came to light. The bank claimed these funds from its customer, whose defence was that as she was led to believe that her income was greater than it actually was, she had changed her position, and consequently had spent more money than she would otherwise have done. The court *held* that the bank was not entitled to recover the £1,108. The bank was in breach of duty in not keeping its customer correctly informed as to the position of her account (see also *United Overseas Bank* v. *Jiwani* (page 75)).

(5) The banker has a duty to collect for the customer's account cheques paid in by the customer.

10 The Protection of Bankers

Both the Bills of Exchange Act, 1882 and the Cheques Act, 1957 contain provisions which afford protection to both a paying and a collecting bank which would otherwise be liable for paying a cheque to, or collecting it for a person who is not the owner.

PROTECTION OF THE PAYING BANKER

At common law if a paying bank pays one of his customer's cheques to a person not entitled to it he will be liable to the true owner in conversion, and, furthermore he cannot debit his customer's account. Statute law, however, provides four possible defences to a banker:

(1) Under s 59, Bills of Exchange Act

It will be recalled (see page 54) that payment of a bill at or after maturity to the holder, payment being made in good faith and without notice of any defect in the holder's title to the bill will discharge the drawee (s 59).

In the present context this section affords a good defence to a paying banker who pays in good faith, etc. the bearer of a *bearer cheque*, even if the bearer is not the person rightfully entitled to the cheque; the bank can properly debit its customer's account.

But payment to the person holding an *order cheque* on which there is a forged or unauthorised indorsement is not a holder because the cheque has not been properly negotiated to him, and the payment to him will not absolve the paying bank from liability.

(2) Under s 60, Bills of Exchange Act

S 60 provides that when a banker pays a cheque drawn on him in good faith and in the ordinary course of business, it is not the duty of the banker to show that the indorsement of the payee or any subsequent indorsement was made by or under the authority of the person whose indorsement it purports to be. The banker is deemed to have paid the bill in due course, although such indorsement has been forged or made without authority. (If the drawer's signature on a bill of exchange is forged the instrument fails

80

to satisfy the basic definition (s 3) of a bill of exchange. The payee or subsequent indorsee will not be entitled to claim payment from the drawee named in the order.)

It was shown in Chapter 4 that where the signature of the payee or a subsequent indorsee is forged, that forged signature is wholly inoperative (s 24). A person who takes a bill after a forged indorsement cannot acquire the status of holder in due course. Such a person is described as a wrongful possessor. The wrongful possessor can only pursue the forger and any subsequent indorsers. If the drawee pays to the wrongful possessor the amount stated in the order he remains liable to the true owner for the same amount.

S 60 thus provides an exception in that protection is given to the drawee where he is a banker and the bill in question 'is payable to order on demand', i.e. a cheque payable to order. Thus:

If Able draws up a bill made payable to Cain on demand and the drawee is the Brown Bank Ltd the bank's liability will be discharged if:

(1) It pays Cain; or

(2) It pays a subsequent indorsee.

In neither case is the Brown Bank required to investigate the indorsements on the bill to ensure their validity. The bank will be deemed to have paid the bill in due course and will be discharged from liability notwithstanding any forged or unauthorised indorsements on that bill.

The bill drawn by Able to Cain may on its reverse side contain the following indorsements:

Pay to the order of Quentin

        Cain (Signature forged by Mark who
        stole the cheque from Cain)

Pay to the order of Xavier
  Quentin (Signature)

The indorsement by Mark is a forgery and is therefore inoperative. Title to the bill does not therefore pass to Quentin who has no title to pass to Xavier.

If the bill does not satisfy the requirements of s 60 by either (1) not being drawn on a banker, or (2) not being a bill payable to order on demand, then payment by the drawee to Xavier will not discharge the liability of the drawee and he will remain liable to Cain, the true owner of the bill.

If the bill is payable to order on demand and drawn on a banker then payment by the banker to Xavier, by virtue of s 60, will discharge the banker from any further liability. Brown Bank Ltd is entitled to debit Able's account and will not be liable in conversion to the true owner of the cheque, Cain. Furthermore, Able is deemed to have paid his debt to Cain, so long as the cheque actually reached the payee and was not stolen before it reached Cain. Cain's remedies will be against Quentin and Xavier who have no title to the cheque.

In order that a banker obtains the protection of s 60 he must also (a) pay the cheque in the ordinary course of business, and (b) pay the cheque in good faith:

(a) A bank would not be paying in the ordinary course of business if, for example:
  (i) Payment was made after banking hours.

BAINES v. NATIONAL PROVINCIAL BANK LTD (1927) 32 Com Cas 216

A cheque was presented and paid by the bank five minutes after closing time. The drawer countermanded payment when the bank opened the following morning but the bank had already debited his account. The drawer claimed that the bank had paid the cheque outside of its advertised business time and that consequently the payment was not in the ordinary course of business. The court *held* that the bank is allowed a reasonable period after its advertised closing time to complete its business and that the bank had acted within its rights in cashing the cheque.

(ii) A bank has paid cash over the bank counter on a crossed cheque. The practice of crossing cheques has arisen in order to give some protection to the drawer in that he may have time to stop the cheque while it is being cleared or while it is being negotiated by the person who stole it.

(b) A bank will rarely act in bad faith. If a bank knows that an indorsement is forged it will refuse to pay. Similarly if a banker has received notice of a certain cheque payable to order being lost or stolen it will refuse to pay the amount stated in the order to the person presenting the cheque for payment.

(3) Under s 80, Bills of Exchange Act (crossed cheques)

S 80 provides that where the banker on whom a crossed cheque is drawn in good faith and without negligence pays it, if crossed generally, to a banker, and if crossed specially to the banker to whom it is crossed (or his agent for collection being a banker) the banker paying the cheque, and, if the cheque has come into the hands of the payee, the drawer, shall respectively be entitled to the same rights and be placed in the same position as if payment of the cheque had been made to the true owner of it.

Thus in the event of a banker paying a crossed cheque to another banker in accordance with the crossing, in good faith, and without negligence he is discharged from liability with respect to that cheque. In these circumstances the drawer has no right of action against the drawee provided that the drawee has acted in accordance with the crossing. If the cheque has at some time come into the hands of the payee the drawer's liability to the payee is also discharged. Thus:

> Able has drawn a cheque on Brown Bank Ltd in favour of Cain: when Cain receives the cheque he crosses it generally; the cheque is then stolen from Cain by Mark who goes to Smith Bank Ltd, pretends that he is Cain and opens an account at Smith Bank Ltd in the name of Cain. Payment of the cheque by Brown Bank Ltd to Smith Bank Ltd will discharge Brown Bank's liability despite the fact that Mark had no title and Able's account can be duly debited.
>
> Similarly, once Able has delivered the cheque to Cain, even if payment is made to Mark and not to Cain, Able's liability to Cain is discharged. Able is entitled to be placed in the same position as if payment had been made to Cain.

Neither s 60 nor s 80 protects a banker who pays a cheque on which its customer's signature as drawer is forged or if the cheque has been materially altered.

All other protection afforded to bankers is provided by the Cheques Act, 1957.

(4) Under s 1, Cheques Act

S 1 of the Cheques Act, 1957 provides that where a banker in good faith and in the ordinary course of business pays a cheque drawn on him which is not indorsed or is irregularly indorsed he does not incur any liability by reason only of the absence of, or irregularity in, indorsement. The banker is deemed to have paid in due course.

By s 1(2) the above provision is extended to orders written by a customer to his bank; in other words, cheques made payable 'to cash', dividend warrants and to bankers' drafts.

S 1 implements the recommendations of the Mocatta Committee which was intent on discovering ways to cut down the futile practice of requiring the indorsement of cheques by the payee, who pays the cheque into his own bank account. A bank will obtain a good title to a cheque paid into the account for credit of the payee notwithstanding the bill not being indorsed to the bank or there being an irregular indorsement (e.g. cheque payable to D. Kay indorsed by that person as 'Don Kay'). Indorsement is still required by bankers where the payee or his transferee presents an uncrossed cheque across the counter for cash and also, of course, where the payee negotiates the cheque (in which case the indorsement of all but the person who presents the cheque for collection, is required). Thus:

> If Cain pays a cheque into his bank account at the Smith Bank he will not be required to indorse the cheque to the bank. Despite the absence of an indorsement the bank will obtain a good title to the cheque. Cain would have to indorse the cheque if he 'negotiated' it to anyone other than a banker. Cain, for example, would have to indorse the cheque if he wanted to negotiate the cheque to his Building Society.
>
> To take a more difficult example: assume that Able draws an order cheque on Brown Bank Ltd in favour of Cain and the cheque is stolen from Cain, the payee, by Mark. Mark now opens an account in Cain's name at Smith Bank Ltd and Brown Bank pays the amount of the cheque to Smith Bank. Now, despite the fact that Smith Bank has not required its 'customer' Mark, to indorse the cheque before collecting it for him, so long as Brown Bank has acted in good faith and in the ordinary course of business it will be entitled to debit Able's account.

S 3 of the Cheques Act, 1957 further provides that an unindorsed cheque which appears to have been paid by the banker on whom it is drawn is evidence of the receipt by the payee of the sum payable by the cheque. Thus it is the appearance of the cheque which determines whether payment has been made by the payee.

PROTECTION OF THE COLLECTING BANKER

(1) Collecting bank 'as holder' in due course

S 2, Cheques Act, 1957 provides that a banker who gives value for, or has a lien on a cheque, payable to order which the holder delivers to him for collection, without indorsing it, has such rights as he would have had if, upon delivery, the holder had indorsed it in blank.

This section aims to provide protection for the collecting banker. The holder who delivers a cheque to him will be a customer of that bank; the

84

bank is acting as agent for his customer by collecting the amount stated in the order from the bank named in the order, the paying banker. The banker is protected by s 2 with respect to cheques payable to order notwithstanding the absence of an indorsement to the bank which would otherwise preclude the banker from qualifying as the legal holder of the cheque.

Protection is given to the collecting banker provided either

(a) He gives value for the cheque, or

(b) He has a lien on the cheque.

(a) Value given by collecting banker

Whenever the banker gives value for a cheque and fulfils all the particulars of the definition of a holder in due course, then despite the *absence of* an indorsement (*not* where there is a *forged* or irregular indorsement), the banker will escape liability for conversion if he collects payment of a cheque for a person who is not the true owner; he will obtain a good title, even if he could not, by reason of his negligence, shelter behind the protection given by s 4 (see below), and can sue the drawer of the cheque if it is dishonoured.

A banker may give value for a cheque in four ways:

(i) By cashing or exchanging a cheque for a customer or any other holder. The banker is giving something in return for the cheque, there is consideration for the transaction, the banker has thereby given value for the cheque.

(ii) By taking a cheque from a customer for the express purpose of reducing the customer's overdraft. An overdraft is a debt owed by a customer to his banker. Reducing an overdraft is valuable consideration for the taking of a cheque.

M'LEAN v. CLYDESDALE BANKING CO. (1883) 9 App Cas 95

A customer of C bank had overdrawn on his account. The customer was given a cheque by M which he paid into his account in order to reduce his overdraft. M then stopped the cheque. The House of Lords *held* that C bank had given value for the cheque by reducing the overdraft and that the C bank could therefore recover the amount of the cheque from M.

(iii) By expressly or impliedly agreeing to allow a customer to draw against the value of uncleared cheques paid into the account. By so agreeing the banker is giving the customer a facility of value. The banker therefore gives valuable consideration in exchange for the receipt of the cheques.

(iv) By paying cheques against uncleared items as a matter of practice. The bank is giving a customer a financial facility by paying cheques despite the fact that cheques paid into the account have not been cleared.

WESTMINSTER BANK LTD v. ZANG [1966] AC 182

Zang, being short of cash, asked T for £1,000 in cash in return for a cheque. T agreed. The cash was paid by T Ltd (of which T was managing director) from its account at the W Bank but the cheque drawn by Z was payable to T personally. T paid the cheque (which was unindorsed) into the account of T Ltd. On presentation for payment Z's cheque was dishonoured. The W Bank brought an action against Z claiming to be holders for value of the cheque by virtue of s 2, Cheques Act, 1957. The House of Lords *held* that the bank had not given value for the cheque. The fact that the account was overdrawn did not amount to the giving of value by the bank since interest was charged on the original amount of the overdraft unreduced by the cheque, and there was no evidence of an agreement to allow the company to draw against uncleared cheques. The W Bank had not given value for the cheque and could therefore not succeed in their action against Zang.

S 2 allows an order cheque to be negotiated without indorsement, but, unlike s 4 (below), applies only to cheques and not to 'analogous instruments'.

(b) Collecting banker's lien

A banker will have a lien on a cheque which was originally received for collection and has been returned unpaid, it now being discovered that the customer's balance is insufficient to meet the unpaid debit. More generally a banker has by implication of law a lien on all bills or cheques which come into his hands in the course of his business as a banker to the extent of the sum owing to him by his customer. By s 27(3), where the holder of a bill has a lien on it arising either from contract or by implication of law, he is deemed to be a holder for value to the extent of the sum for which he has a lien.

(2) Under s 4, Cheques Act, 1957

S 4 of the Cheques Act, 1957 provides that where a banker in good faith and without negligence

(a) Receives payment for a customer, or

(b) Having credited a customer's account, receives payment for himself:

86

then even if the customer has no title or a defective title to the instrument, the banker does not incur any liability to the true owner of the instrument, by reason only of having received payment.

This section protects the bank from the tort of conversion; otherwise a banker would be liable to the true owner for converting his property for the use of the bank.

The section applies not only to cheques but also to orders made payable 'to cash', bankers drafts, dividend warrants, and certain public documents which enable the holder to claim payment from the Paymaster General, or from the Queen's and Lord Treasurer's Remembrancer.

The collecting bank is only protected under s 4 when collecting for 'a customer', i.e. a person who keeps an account with the bank; the relationship of banker and customer will also arise when an account is opened by paying in a cheque which is accepted for collection: in the absence of negligence, e.g. as to obtaining references (see Chapter 9), the collecting bank will be protected in respect of the first cheque.

Lord Dunedin, in *Taxation Commissioners* v. *English, Scottish & Australian Bank* [1920] AC 683, said:

> 'The word 'customer' signifies a relationship in which duration is not of the essence. . . . The contract is not between an habitué and a newcomer, but between a person for whom the bank performs a casual service, such as, for instance, cashing a cheque for a person introduced by one of their customers and a person who has an account of his own at the bank'.

S 4 requires that the banker collects in good faith and without negligence, but a banker is not to be treated for the purposes of this section as negligent by reason only of his failure to concern himself with the absence of, or irregularity in, indorsement of an instrument. Thus:

> If Able draws up a cheque payable to Cain which Cain presents to his own bank, the Smith Bank, they will collect the proceeds from the Brown Bank and credit Cain's account with that amount. There is no need for Cain to indorse the cheque to the bank. Provided that the Smith Bank acts in good faith and without negligence they will never be liable for the tort of conversion.

Negligence with respect to collecting cheques may be founded upon any departure from the standard of care required by the practice of bankers. A banker will be negligent (and therefore is not protected against liability in conversion) if he pays a given cheque in a situation where previous and present events are out of the ordinary and ought to raise doubts in a banker's mind and so put him on enquiry with respect to that cheque. The following cases serve to illustrate some of the possible negligent acts of the collecting banker. (Reference should also be made to the cases of *Ladbroke* v. *Todd*, *Hampstead Guardians* v. *Barclays Bank Ltd*, and *Marfani & Co.* v. *Midland Bank Ltd*, discussed in Chapter 9.)

A.L. UNDERWOOD LTD v. BANK OF LIVERPOOL [1924] 1 KB 775

The bank failed to enquire when a company director paid a cheque drawn for the benefit of the company into his own account having indorsed the cheque to himself. The bankers were *held* to be negligent.

ROSS v. LONDON COUNTY WESTMINSTER & PARR'S BANK [1919] 1 KB 678

A public official paid a cheque made payable to himself in his public capacity into his personal bank account. The bank failed to enquire and was *held* to be negligent.

LLOYDS BANK LTD v. SAVORY & CO. [1933] AC 201

A bank collected, without inquiry, numerous cheques payable 'to bearer' drawn by a stockbroking firm intended to be paid to jobbers. The bank was collecting in one case for an employee of the firm and in the other case for the wife of another employee. The bank was *held* to be negligent and could not therefore recover the money. In delivering his judgement Lord Wright said: 'The most obvious circumstances which should put the banker on his guard (apart from manifest irregularities in the indorsement and such like) are where a cheque is presented for collection which bears on its face a warning that the customer may have misappropriated it, as for instance where a customer known to be a servant or agent pays in for collection a cheque drawn by third parties in favour of his employer or principal . . . I think . . . that at least where the new customer is employed in some position which involves his handling, and having the opportunity of stealing, his employer's cheques, the bankers fail in taking adequate precautions if they do not ask the name of his employers . . . because they fail to ascertain a most relevant fact as to the intending customer's circumstances.'

Similarly, in *Marquess of Bute* v. *Barclays Bank Ltd* [1955] 1 QB 202 the bank was *held* to be negligent when collecting for the private account of an agent cheques obviously intended for his principal.

In other circumstances banks have, of course, been held not to be negligent.

88

SLINGSBY v. WESTMINSTER BANK LTD [1931] 1 KB 173

A bank manager made enquiries of a solicitor paying in a cheque. The answers received were consistent with information previously received. The bankers were *held* not to be negligent.

ORBIT MINING CO. LTD v. WESTMINSTER BANK LTD [1963] 1 QB 794

The plaintiff company had an account with the Midland Bank on which any two directors could sign. One of the directors was often abroad, so on occasions he signed a number of cheque forms in blank intending their being used for the company's business. The remaining director made the cheques payable 'To cash or order', countersigned them with his own illegible signature, indorsed them and paid them into his personal account at the Westminster Bank for collection. The instruments, although not cheques, were within the protection afforded by s 4 of the Cheques Act. The Court of Appeal *held* that the bankers were not negligent and the company was therefore unable to recover the money from the Westminster Bank. The fact that the instruments were drawn 'to cash or order' was not in itself enough to give rise to suspicion; furthermore, the collecting bank was unaware of the connection between their customer and the company; their customer's signature on the cheque was illegible and there was nothing to indicate to the collecting bank that he was in any way concerned with the drawing of the cheque.

By s 11 of the Torts (Interference with Goods) Act, 1977, contributory negligence was no longer available as a defence to conversion. Thus if the collecting bank lost the protection of s 4 by virtue of its negligence, the damages it had to pay the true owner of the cheque by virtue of having converted it was not reduced by any contributory negligence on the part of the owner of the cheque.

However, s 47, Banking Act, 1979 restores to bankers the defence afforded by s 4, Cheques Act, 1957 where the bank is pleading contributory negligence.

11 Promissory Notes

A promissory note is defined by s 83 as an unconditional promise in writing made by one person to another signed by the maker, engaging to pay on demand or at a fixed determinable future time a sum certain in money to or to the order of a specified person or to bearer.

A promissory note only involves two parties. It will be recalled that a bill of exchange involves essentially three parties, the drawer, the drawee and the payee. With respect to promissory notes, the drawer and drawee are the same person and are described as 'the maker'. The maker engages to pay a sum certain in money to or to the order of a specified person or to the bearer of the note at its maturity. Thus:

£500   25 Long Street, London

28 December 1980

Three months after date I promise to pay Cain or order
the sum of five hundred pounds for value received

        (signed)
                Able

Able is the maker of this promissory note, and Cain is the payee.

S 89 states that the provisions in the Act relating to bills of exchange apply, with the necessary modifications as stated in Part IV of the Act (s 83-9), to promissory notes.

The maker of the note, Able, in our example, is deemed to correspond with the acceptor of a bill, and the first indorser of a note shall be deemed to correspond with the drawer of an accepted bill payable to drawer's order (s 89(2)).

An instrument in the form of a note payable to maker's order but which is not indorsed by the maker is not a promissory note (s 83(2)). Once the maker has indorsed the instrument either by indorsement in blank or by special indorsement, delivery will render the maker liable on the note.

To facilitate the giving of promissory notes as security for loans, the notes often being accompanied by the deposit of shares or title deeds, s 83(3) provides that a note is not invalid by reason that it contains a pledge of collateral security with authority to sell or dispose of that security in order to satisfy the promise in the note.

INLAND AND FOREIGN NOTES

If the note on its face is both drawn and payable within the British Islands it is an inland note. The British Islands are defined in s 4 to include any part of the United Kingdom of Great Britain and Northern Ireland, the islands of Man, Guernsey, Jersey, Alderney, Sark and the islands adjacent to any of them being part of the dominions of Her Majesty. If a note is drawn or payable otherwise than within the British Islands it is a foreign note.

Where a foreign note is dishonoured a protest is unnecessary (s 89(4)), but since it is common for foreign law to require protest, this procedure is advisable when a note is to be sued on in a foreign court.

THE MAKER OF A NOTE

There may be two or more makers of a promissory note and they may be liable jointly or jointly and severally. Joint liability entitles the payee (or subsequent indorsee) to only one attempt at suing the makers for non-payment and thus all the makers must be pursued in the same action, otherwise if in the first action he fails to recover the full amount of the note he will be unable now to claim against other makers not joined in the first action. If the liability is joint and several the payee may pursue any of the makers, and this pursuit will not preclude a future action against any of the other makers. The holder is, of course, always entitled to claim the full amount of the note from any person who has signed the note as a maker, and not merely for his share; a party compelled to pay has a right of contribution from other makers. S 85(2) provides that where a note runs 'I promise to pay' and is signed by two or more persons, it is deemed to be their joint and several note. On the other hand, if the note reads 'We promise' and is signed by two or more makers their liability is joint only.

The maker of a promissory note by making it engages that he will pay it according to the amount stated and date stated in the note, and he is estopped from denying to a holder in due course the existence of the payee and his then capacity to indorse. Thus in the event of dishonour it is not open for the maker to claim that the note is invalid by reason of the payee being a non-existent person or not having the capacity to indorse the note and therefore effectively negotiate the note.

TIME OF PAYMENT

A promissory note may be drawn payable either:

(1) On demand, or

(2) At a fixed future time, or

(3) At a determinable future time.

Where a note is drawn payable on demand and is indorsed it must be presented for payment within a reasonable time from that indorsement. If the note is not presented within a reasonable time the indorser is discharged from liability. Thus the maker will be discharged if the note is not presented to him for payment within a reasonable time from indorsement. The same principle will be applied with respect to any subsequent indorsers. The maker, however, will remain liable for the six-year limitation period from the date when the note matures.

The definition of a reasonable amount of time is to be determined by the nature of the instrument, the trade in which the instrument is used and the facts of the particular case.

S 86(3) provides that where a note payable on demand is negotiated it is not deemed to be overdue because it appears that a reasonable time for presenting the note has elapsed since its issue. Thus even if it appears that more than a reasonable amount of time has elapsed between the issue of the note and its negotiation to him, the holder's title to the note is not defective unless he was given notice of any particular defect. This places the holder of a demand note in a better position than the holder of a demand bill who cannot be a holder in due course of a bill with the ability to take 'free from equities' if the bill has been in circulation for more than a reasonable time and which is therefore 'overdue'.

PRESENTMENT FOR PAYMENT

A note need not be presented for acceptance nor need it be accepted. S 89(3) provides that the provisions as to bills with respect to presentment for acceptance and the act of acceptance itself do not apply to promissory notes.

Presentment for payment is not necessary in order to render the maker liable unless the note is made payable at a particular place. If, however, a note is made payable at a particular place it must be presented for payment at that place in order to render the maker and indorser liable (s 87).

Where a place of payment is indicated by way of memorandum only, presentment at that place is sufficient to render the indorser liable, but a presentment to the maker elsewhere, provided it is sufficient in other respects, will also be adequate (s 87).

A note must always be presented for payment so as to render the indorser of the note liable (s 87 (2)), i.e. within a reasonable time of the indorsement in the case of a demand note and on the last day for payment in the case of a time note.

DISTINCTIONS BETWEEN PROMISSORY NOTES AND BILLS OF EXCHANGE

(1) A note is a promise to pay, whereas a bill is an order to pay.

(2) The maker of a note is always primarily liable and corresponds to the acceptor of a bill. The drawer of a bill, once the bill has been accepted, is only liable as a surety in the event of the acceptor dishonouring a bill by non-payment.

(3) Notes cannot be issued in sets (s 89(3)d). Bills may be drawn in sets.

(4) Notes are never accepted. Bills drawn payable after sight or drawn payable elsewhere than at the residence or place of business of the drawee must be presented for acceptance. A bill may also expressly provide that it must be accepted before it can be presented for payment.

(5) Makers of a note may be liable jointly or jointly and severally as prescribed by the note. Acceptors of a bill, if more than one, must be liable jointly.

(6) Foreign notes do not require protesting. Foreign bills require protesting in the event of dishonour for non-acceptance or non-payment.

BANK NOTES

A bank note is a variety of promissory note issued by a banker and payable to bearer on demand, the sum stated in the note.

Bank notes are issued by the Bank of England and can only be drawn for the amounts approved by the Treasury. Bank of England notes are regarded as legal tender in England and Wales; promissory notes are merely instruments enabling the payment of a debt to be delayed. Promissory notes are not legal tender. Bank notes are never statute-barred whereas promissory notes are subject to the Statute of Limitation.

In *Suffell* v. *Bank of England* (1882) 9 QBD 555, Jessell M.R. said:

'A Bank of England note is not an ordinary commercial contract to pay money. It is, in one sense, a promissory note in terms, but no one can describe it as simply a promissory note. It is part of the currency of the country. It has long been made so by Act of Parliament.'

I.O.U.s

An I.O.U. is simply an acknowledgement of a debt, and, without more, cannot be a promissory note: of course, if the I.O.U. contains additional words that amount to a promise to pay the debt (as distinct from a mere acknowledgement) then it may well be a promissory note.

Index to Statutes

Banker's Books Evidence Act, 1879, 78
Banking Act, 1979, s 47, 89
Banking and Financial Dealings Act,
   1971, 18
Bills of Exchange Act, 1882
  s 2, 15, 58, 81
  s 3, 14, 35, 54, 58, 59
  s 3(2), 15
  s 3(3), 15
  s 4, 91
  s 5(2), 23
  s 6, 16
  s 7, 19
  s 7(3), 20, 21
  s 8(1), 35
  s 8 (3), 20
  s 8(5), 10
  s 9(1), 19
  s 9(2), 19
  s 9(3), 19
  s 10, 17
  s 10(2), 41
  s 10(3), 17
  s 11, 17
  s 12, 41
  s 13(2), 18
  s 16, 35
  s 17(1), 40
  s 17(2), 40
  s 18(3), 41
  s 19(2), 42
  s 20, 38
  s 21, 40
  s 21(1), 37
  s 21(3), 37
  s 23, 29, 32, 40
  s 24, 31, 81
  s 26(2), 30
  s 27, 24
  s 27(2), 27
  s 27(3), 28, 86
  s 28, 43
  s 29(1), 25
  s 29(2), 26
  s 29(3), 25, 28
  s 30(1), 28

s 30(2), 28
s 31, 34
s 32, 34, 35
s 33, 35
s 34(1), 35
s 34(2), 35
s 36, 18
s 36(5), 47
s 40, 41
s 41, 41, 42
s 43, 42
s 44, 42
s 45, 44, 45
s 46, 45
s 47, 46
s 49(3), 48
s 49(4), 48
s 50, 50
s 51(1), 51
s 51(2), 51
s 51(7), 51
s 51(9), 52
s 52(1), 45
s 54(2), 43
s 55(2), 36
s 56, 29
s 57, 52
s 58(2), 37
s 59, 80
s 59(1), 54
s 59(3), 54, 55
s 60, 75, 80, 81, 82, 83
s 61, 54, 55
s 62, 54, 56
s 63, 54, 56
s 64, 54, 57
s 71(1), 12
s 71(2), 13
s 71(5), 13
s 73, 58, 59, 61
s 74, 60
s 76, 65
s 77(5), 69
s 77(6), 69
s 78, 69
s 79(1), 66

s 79(2), 65, 66, 69
s 80, 75, 83
s 81, 68
s 83, 90
s 85(2), 91
s 86(3), 92
s 87, 92, 93
s 89, 90
s 89(3), 90, 92
s 89(4), 91
s 90, 26
s 91, 29
s 92, 18
s 94, 52

Cheques Act, 1959
s 1, 83, 84
s 1(2), 83
s 2, 84, 85, 86

s 3, 84
s 4, 85, 86, 87, 89
Carriage Act, 1870, 15
Companies Act, 1948
s 33, 29
s 108(4), 29

Judicature Act, 1873, s 25, 2, 4
Judicature Act, 1925, s 47, 36

Law of Property Act, 1925, s 136, 2, 4,
26

Sale of Goods Act, 1979, s 2, 23
Statute of Limitation, 1939, 59, 71

Tort (Interference with Goods) Act,
1971, s 11, 89

Index to Cases

Baines v. National Provincial Bank Ltd,
    82
Bank of England v. Vagliano Bros, 21,
    32
Barclays Bank Ltd v. W.J. Sims & Son
    and Cooke (Southern) Ltd and
    Sowman (1979), 61
Bavins Junior & Sims v. London & South
    Western Bank, 15
Bechuanaland Exploration Co. v.
    London Trading Bank, 8
Brewer v. Westminster Bank Ltd, 77
Burnett v. Westminster Bank Ltd, 61

Clutton v. Attenborough & Sons, 21, 31
Curtice v. London City & Midland Bank,
    61

Davidson v. Barclays Bank Ltd, 76
Diamond v. Graham, 27

Eagle Hill Ltd v. Needham Builders Ltd,
    49
Elliot v. Bax-Ironside, 30

Gibbons v. Westminster Bank Ltd, 76
Greenwood v. Martins Bank Ltd, 75

Hamilton Finance v. Coverley, Westray
    & Others, 49
Hampstead Guardians v. Barclays Bank,
    72, 88
Hibernian Bank Ltd v. Gysin & Hanson,
    36
Holland v. Manchester & Liverpool
    Banking Co., 75

Jackson v. White and Midland Bank Ltd,
    78
Joachimson v. Swiss Bank Corporation
    71, 73
Jones v. Waring & Gillow Ltd, 25

Ladbroke & Co. v. Todd, 72, 88
Liggett (Liverpool) Ltd v. Barclays Bank
    Ltd, 77

Lloyds Bank Ltd v. Brooks, 79
Lloyds Bank Ltd v. Cooke, 39
Lloyds Bank Ltd v. Savory & Co., 88
London Joint Stock Bank v. MacMillan
    & Arthur, 57, 74
London Provincial & South Western
    Bank Ltd v, Buszard, 61
London River Plate Bank v. Bank of
    Liverpool, 33

Marfani & Co. v. Midland Bank Ltd, 72,
    88
Marquess of Bute v. Barclays Bank Ltd,
    88
M'Lean v. Clydesdale Banking Co., 85
Morison v. Kemp, 30

National Westminster Bank Ltd v.
    Barclays Bank International Ltd, 77
North & South Insurance Corp. v.
    National Provincial Bank Ltd, 58
North & South Wales Bank Ltd v.
    Macbeth, 22

Oliver v. Davis & Woodcock, 24
Orbit Mining Co. Ltd v. Westminster
    Bank Ltd, 89

Pollway v. Abdullah, 24

Ross v. London County Westminster &
    Parr's Bank, 88

Slingsby v. District Bank Ltd, 74, 89
Re Soltykoff, Ex parte Margrett, 23
Suffell v. Bank of England, 93

Taxation Commissioners v. English,
    Scottish & Australian Bank, 87
Tournier v. National Provincial & Union
    Bank of England, 78

A.L. Underwood Ltd v. Bank of
    Liverpool, 88
United Overseas Bank v. Jiwani, 75, 79

Vinden v. Hughes, 21, 22, 31

Westminster Bank Ltd v. Zang, 86
Williamson v. Rider, 18

Yeoman Credit Ltd v. Gregory, 45
Young v. Grote, 74

General Index

acceptance, 12, 40
  accommodation party, by, 43
  agent by, 42
  dated, 41
  effect of, 43
  general, 42
  honour for, 52
  noting and protesting, 12
  partial, 43
  presentment for, 41
  qualified, 42
  types of, 42
accommodation party, 43
  payment by, 55
agent, 30
  acceptance by, 42
  bank as, 62, 73
  bill dishonoured in hands of, 47
assignment
  debt, of, 5
  equities subject to, 2
  legal, recognition of, 3
  life policy, of, 4

bank, 58
  agent, as, 73
  bad faith, acting in, 82
  cheques and (*see* cheque)
    collect, duty to, 79
    crossed to, 69
    honour, duty to, 76
      termination of, 62
    lien on, having, 86
  collecting, protection of, 84
  contributory negligence, pleading, 89
  conversion, protected from, 80, 87
  crossed cheque, paying to the banker, 83
  customer, and, 71
    death of, 62
    duty of, 74
    duty to, 75
    keeping informed, 78
  defences available to, 80
  deposit account, 72
  disclosure, requiring, 78

  duty and authority of, 60
  duty owed by, 75
  duty owed to, 74
  holder in due course, as, 84
  insolvent, becoming, 60
  investigation of indorsement by, 80
  joint account, 77
  negligence of, 72, 87
  ordinary course of business, paying in, 82
  protection of, 80 *et seq*.
  secret, duty to keep, 78
  statutory protection, 75
banker's draft, 16
bank note, 93
bearer, 20
bill of exchange, 2
  acceptance of, *see* acceptance
  alteration of, 57
  bearer, 10, 37
    delivery, negotiated by, 37
  cancellation of, 56
  codification of law, 8
  consideration for, 24
  contingency, payable on, 17
  contact, as, 23
  defect on, 27
  delivery of, *see* delivery
  discharge of, see discharge
  discounting, 6
  dishonoured, *see also* notice of dishonour
    damages on, 52
    non-payment, for, 46
  example of, 5
  foreign, 11, 51
  future, payable in, 9
  holder of, 25, *and see* holder
    waiver of rights, 56
  inland, 11
  meaning, 5, 14, 35
  not negotiable, 35
  omission on, 38
  operation of, 9
  order, 11, 34
    transferred for value, 36

overdue, 26
    negotiated, 36
payable on demand, 16, 17
payable to bearer, converting to, 10
payment of, *see* payment
'per pro', signed, 30
promissory note, distinguished, 93
restrictive indorsement, 68
set of, 12
sighting, 9, 10
signature on, *see* signature
specified person, payable to, 19
sum payable to be certain, 18
'time', 18
transfer
    delivery, by, 3
    notice of, 4
    of title, 26
unconditional order, stating, 15
value given for, 3
writing, to be in, 15
British Islands, definition of, 11

cheque, 7
    bank, and, *and see* bank
        collected by, 79
        duty to honour, 76
        giving value for, 85
        lien on, 86
    careless, 74
    cash, payable to, 73
    countermand, 61
    crossing, 63, 65 *et seq.*
        'account payee', 67
        after issue, 68
        alteration to, 69
        banker, by, 69
        banker paying to other banker, 83
        general, 65
        'not negotiable', 68
        rules as to, 69
        special, 66
        type of, 65
    date on, 59
    delay in presenting, 60
    forgery of, 76
    form of, 63
    indorsement of, 80
        investigation of, 80
        irregularity in, 83
        requirement of, 84
    joint account, on, 77
    lost or stolen, 82
    meaning, 59
    nature of, 58 *et seq.*
    negligence in collecting, 87
    negotiated, 68
    other bills, distinguished, 63

payable on demand, 17
payable to self, 20
post-dated, 57
stolen, 72
travellers', 59
unsigned, 77
wrongful dishonour of, 76
chose in action, 1
    transferee suing in own name, 2
computer
    banking, use in, 63
contingency
    bill payable on, 17
consideration, 24
    illegal, 27
contract
    banker and customer, between, 71
    bill as, 23
    capacity to, 23
    consideration, 24
    person not party to, enforcing, 1
    undertaking to pay money, 1
corporation, capacity of, 23

damages
    dishonoured bill, on, 52
debenture, 7
debt
    antecedent, 24
    bankers, by, 71
    bill evidencing, 23
    i.o.u. acknowledging, 94
    past, 24
delivery, 37
    effectual, 37
    inchoate bill, of, 38
    meaning, 37
discharge, 54 *et seq.*
    renunciation, by, 56
dividend warrant, 7
drawee, 14
    acceptance by, 40
    bill, to be named in, 16
    cheque, of, 58
    dead, 42
    fictitious, 16, 23, 46
    joint, presentment to, 41
    partners, 16
    signing bill, 16
drawer, 14
    bankrupt, 48
    cheque, of, 58
    dead, 48
    drawee, to address bill to, 16
    fictitious, 51
    joint, 48
    no capacity, having, 51
duress, 27

estoppel, 39

forgery, 30 *et seq.*
    cheque of, 76
    signature on cheque of, 75
        one party to joint account, by, 77
    wife, by, 33
fraud, 26
foreign exchange control, 6

garnishee order
    bank account, freezing, 62

holder, 25
    acceptor becoming, 55
    benefits, gaining, 26
    indorser negotiating authority to, 35
    in due course, 25
        bank as, 84
    liability of party, cancelling, 56
    meaning, 25, 28
    presentment for payment by, 44
    rights, renouncing, 56
    value for, 27
    waiver of rights, 56

indorsement
    blank, in, 10, 11, 34
    conditional, 35
    effect of, 36
    restrictive, 35
    rules, 34
    set, of, 13
    special, 35
    specific, 11
instalments, 19
interest, bill payable with, 18, 19

life assurance policy, 4

Mocatta Committee, 84
mistake
    bill, when signing, 29

negotiability, 2
negotiable instrument
    characteristics of, 3
non-business day, 18
notice of dishonour, 46 *et seq.*
    delay of, 50
    dispensed with, where, 50
    effect of, 47
    form of, 48
    not received, 50
    recipient of, 48

    time for, 49
    who may give, 47
noting and protesting, 51

overdraft, 71

payee, 14
    fictitious, 20
    joint, 20
    non-existing, 21
    types of, 20
payment, 4, 44
    cheque, of
        countermanding, 61
        customer's order on, 76
    delay, 45
    discharge by, 54
    honour, for, 53
    in due course, 54
    non-, 46
    promissory note, of, 92
    rules as to presentment, 44
    time for, 45
promissory note, 6, 16, 90
    bank note as, 7, 93
    bills of exchange
        distinguished, 93
    foreign, 91
    inland, 91
    i.o.u., not, 94
    maker of, 90, 91
    payment of, 92
    presentment of, 92
    security for loan, as, 91

security
    bill of exchange as, 6
set of bills, 12
    indorsement to different people, 13
share certificate, 47
signature, 29
    authority, made by, 29
    forged, 30
        wife, by, 33
    partnerships, of, 29
    procuration, by, 30
    unauthorised, 30
Statute of Limitation, 71
subrogation, 77

title
    defect in, 26

waiver
    holder's rights, of, 56